Russia *and the* USSR *1905–56*

JOHN LAVER

Hodder & Stoughton

A MEMBER OF THE HODDER HEADLINE GROUP

The Russian Empire in 1905

How backward was pre-revolutionary Russia? How was Russia governed, and how effective a ruler was the Tsar?

A The Russian Empire in 1905.

Source A shows one of the important differences between Russia and Britain or indeed any other European country at the beginning of the twentieth century: its size. If you had travelled across the Russian Empire in 1905 from Vladivostock on the Pacific coast to the Russian capital St Petersburg, the journey would have taken a week. This was not because the famous Trans-Siberian Railway was particularly inefficient, it was just that Russia was a huge size. In fact, the Russian Empire made up one-sixth of the total land size of the world.

Less than half the population of the Empire was Russian: the rest were other peoples who had been conquered and still had their own languages and often their own religions. The most powerful church in the Empire was a Christian one, the Russian Orthodox Church. It was supported by the government and owned much land.

Amongst some of the conquered peoples there was a desire to get their freedom back. This was particularly true in the west of the Russian Empire, where peoples such as the Poles and the Finns had once been nations in their own right.

The political system

Another difference between Russia and Britain was the way in which they were governed. In Britain in 1905 most men, although no women, could elect people to parliament, which made laws. However, Russia was an **autocracy**. This means that it was ruled by one man, who had almost total power. He was Tsar Nicholas II. He had no parliament to block or to carry out his wishes. He listened only to the advisers which he appointed, and to his German wife, the Tsarina Alexandra.

The people of the Empire

The Russian Empire was a land of great contrasts. Over 90 per cent of the people were poor peasants, barely able to scratch a living from the land, which they rarely owned themselves. Most were in debt and farmed with old-fashioned tools. Much of the soil was poor, and the climate was harsh. At the other end of the scale was the aristocracy. Most Russian nobles lived comfortably on large estates in the countryside or in St Petersburg. There was also a small **middle class** which increasingly provided many of the civil servants or bureaucrats who carried out the Tsar's orders to run the country. But most people in Russia had little or no schooling.

In two rooms there is complete darkness. The ceiling is so low that a tall man cannot stand upright … The plaster is crumbling, there are holes in the walls stopped up with rags. It is dirty. The stove has collapsed. Swarms of cockroaches and bugs. No double window frames and so it is piercingly cold. The lavatory is so broken down that it is dangerous to enter and children are not allowed in.

Changes in the towns

Compared to most western European countries in 1905, Russia was economically backward. But this situation was beginning to change. Large factories were springing up, often foreign-owned, and Russian industry was growing at a faster rate than any other European country. Large numbers of peasants flocked to the towns to work in the factories. They made up the working class or **proletariat**. Their conditions were terrible. Workers lived in slums or even in the factories, earned low wages, worked long hours, and were forbidden to form trade unions to fight for better conditions. Protests or strikes were crushed by the police or the army. The numbers of workers grew rapidly as more factories were built, particularly in Moscow and St Petersburg.

	Russia	**Germany**	**Britain**
Iron	4.6	16.8	10.4
Steel	4.8	18.3	7.8
Coal	36.0	190.0	292.0
Oil	9.1	0	0

C A comparison between Russia, Germany and Britain in 1914 (production in millions of tonnes).

An obstinate Tsar

There were people from all classes who desperately wanted change. Some, often called liberals, wanted an elected parliament which could pass laws to make Russia a modern, more up-to-date country.

Others wanted more drastic changes, which would spread wealth more evenly and completely alter the way in which Russia was run. These people were revolutionaries, and their ideas will be examined later. But Nicholas II, although full of good intentions, was a weak and obstinate ruler who insisted that he would go on governing just as his forefathers had done. He and his wife believed that they had been chosen by God to rule, and that no one had the right to challenge them.

For all his wealth and power, the Tsar was not a particularly happy man. A devoted father to his five children, he had to live with the fact that his one son and heir, Alexis, suffered from haemophilia. This was, in those days, an incurable blood disease, which made it likely that he would die young.

D Comments made by Nicholas II.

[On becoming Tsar in 1894] What is going to happen to me … I am not prepared to be the Tsar. I never wanted to become one. I know nothing of the business of ruling. I have no idea of even how to talk to ministers.

[In reply to a letter from his wife in 1916 urging him to be a strong ruler] Tender thanks for the severe written scolding. Your poor little weak-willed hubby.

[A declaration made in 1916 when things were going badly for Russia in the First World War] The day of my coronation I took my oath to absolute power. I must leave this oath intact to my son.

Q

1 What information about Russia in 1905 can you get from source A?
2 In what ways, and why, was the Russian Empire backward in comparison to some other European countries? You should find source C helpful in answering this question.
3 Why were conditions for the peasants and workers generally poor?
4 How was Russia governed in 1905?
5 Study source D. Do these quotations contradict each other? What do they suggest to you about Nicholas II?
6 Source B is a government report made at the time. Source D was put together much later by an historian. Is either one of these sources likely to be more reliable or useful as evidence about conditions in Russia at the beginning of the twentieth century?

The 1905 Revolution

What caused the 1905 Revolution? Why did it fail? How important was it?

War in the Far East

Bad harvests and poor living conditions caused strikes and disturbances in Russia in the early 1900s, even though these were illegal. The Tsar decided that a short, victorious war was one way to boost the prestige of his government and win the support of his people. The opportunity was at hand. Japan and Russia were quarrelling over who should control Korea and Manchuria in the Far East. War broke out in 1904.

The Russo-Japanese War of 1904–5 was a disaster for Russia. Heavy defeats on land and at sea only increased discontent inside Russia. A series of incidents, which came to be known together as the 1905 Revolution, threatened to overturn the tsarist government.

Bloody Sunday

The most spectacular event of the 1905 Revolution was 'Bloody Sunday'. A huge but peaceful march of ordinary people went to the Tsar's Winter Palace in St Petersburg. They trusted the Tsar, and carried a petition calling upon him to make their lives better. Troops guarding the Palace panicked and opened fire on the marchers, killing and injuring hundreds. The Tsar was not there, but the Russian writer Gorky wrote: 'I believe that this is the beginning of the end of the bloodthirsty Tsar'.

The organiser of the march to the Winter Palace was a priest called Father Gapon. He had actually been a police agent, and when this was discovered later he was murdered by revolutionaries.

A An extract from the workers' petition of 1905.

> We working men and inhabitants of St Petersburg … have come to you, our ruler, in quest of justice and protection. We have become beggars, we have been oppressed … We are treated as slaves … Do not refuse assistance to Your people … End the oppressive behaviour of your officials towards them. Destroy the walls between Yourself and Your people … We have only two ways, either towards liberty and happiness or into the grave.

B
A British cartoon of 1905 (published in *Punch*) showing the Tsar's treatment of the petitioners.

THE CZAR OF ALL THE RUSSIAS.

Revolution

In the Black Sea, the crew of the Russian battleship *Potemkin* **mutinied**, mainly in protest at their terrible conditions. Strikes broke out elsewhere. In some cities, workers elected **soviets** or councils to run local affairs. Leon Trotsky, later to become an important revolutionary, became chairman of the St Petersburg Soviet. The Tsar was in a dilemma. How should he respond to such events?

C A letter from the Tsar to his mother.

> There were only two ways open: to find an energetic soldier to crush the rebellion by sheer force. There would be time to breathe then, but, as likely as not, one would have to use force again in a few months, and that would mean rivers of blood and in the end we should be where we started.
>
> The other way would be to give the people their civil rights, freedom of speech, and press, also to have all the laws confirmed by a State Duma or parliament.

Eventually the Tsar was persuaded by his prime minister Count Witte to publish a document called the October Manifesto. This promised a number of changes or reforms, including a parliament or **Duma**. Many Russians, particularly the educated middle classes, welcomed this. They thought they would be given a say in the running of Russia.

These Russians felt that the Tsar's promise of a parliament and other changes meant that he deserved to go on ruling. They were afraid that if violence continued, it might get out of hand and be turned against others who had wealth and property.

Only a small number of revolutionaries thought that nothing had really changed. They wanted to hold out for the overthrow of the Tsar and more drastic changes to people's lives. But the Tsar's police and soldiers crushed the soviets and order was restored.

D Adapted from the October Manifesto.

The rioting and agitation in the capitals and many localities of our Empire fills our hearts with great and deep grief. The welfare of the Russian Emperor is bound up with the welfare of his people, and its sorrows are his sorrows … We order the Government:

1 To grant to the population the right of free citizenship, freedom of person, conscience, speech and meeting …

3 To make a rule that no law will be passed without the agreement of a State Duma [parliament].

E 'Invasion'. A poster from 1905 showing the crushing of a workers' demonstration in Moscow.

It was a close-run thing but the Tsar had survived, at least for the time being. Would he learn any lessons from the 1905 Revolution? Was it important? Some people did think about what had happened. Some of the Tsar's supporters realised that it was necessary to make some changes if they were to prevent such an outbreak of unrest from

happening again. Some revolutionaries believed that the events had shown that they must rely upon their own efforts in the future and not rely upon support from elsewhere. Some revolutionaries doubted that a revolution would succeed in their lifetime. The 1905 Revolution did show that, as long as the army and police were on the side of the Tsar, it would be difficult to overthrow his regime – that is unless a catastrophe occurred on a much greater scale than even the Russo-Japanese War.

1 Most soldiers stayed loyal to the Tsar and helped to crush the revolutionaries.
2 Many of the middle class and Liberals accepted the Tsar's promises to change things in the October Manifesto.
3 The revolutionaries who wanted to fight were increasingly isolated.
4 The peasants who joined in the disturbances were not organised or led effectively.
5 Firm action by the government after the Manifesto was issued.

F Reasons for the failure of the 1905 Revolution.

1 a) What can you learn from source A about the attitude of the people who marched to the Winter Palace?
   b) In what ways was Bloody Sunday an important event?

2 In source B the cartoonist was obviously using his imagination.
   a) What message was the cartoonist trying to put across?
   b) Is the cartoon fair to the Tsar?
   c) Would a Russian cartoon of this event be a more valuable source about the 1905 Revolution? Explain your answer.

3 What point was the artist trying to make in source E? Is there a similarity between this source and source B?

4 Why was there a revolution in Russia in 1905? The following points will help you with your answer: working conditions and poverty; the desire for change in the political system; the impact of the war with Japan. Include any other points you can think of.

5 What do you think was the most important reason for the failure of the 1905 Revolution? Try to weigh up the reasons against each other. For example, if the peasants had been better organised would they have overthrown a Tsar still supported by the army?

3 *Russia from Revolution to War, 1906–14*

Key Issues

How successfully did the Tsar and his government recover from the 1905 Revolution? What attempts were made to change Russia for the better in the years before the First World War? Had Russia changed significantly by 1914?

The Dumas

Nicholas II carried out at least one of his promises after the 1905 Revolution had been suppressed. He allowed elections to a Duma or parliament. The first Duma was elected in 1906. But the system of electing **deputies** was designed to make sure that landlords and other richer people had the biggest say in who was chosen. The Social Democrats (a revolutionary party) **boycotted** the Duma, and the largest party in the Duma after the elections was the Constitutional Democrats or Kadets. The Kadets wanted more power for the Duma and other changes, but they were not revolutionaries. Even so, when the Duma met Nicholas issued the Fundamental Law, which made it clear that he was still very much in charge, and government ministers had to answer only to him.

Nicholas objected to the Duma proposals for reform and closed the Duma after it had met for 75 days. 200 deputies crossed into Finland and held a protest meeting. The second Duma was elected and met in February 1907. This time some Social Democrats were there. After the Tsar closed down this Duma in June, he and his ministers changed the system of election again to make it even more in favour of the rich: there was a deputy for every 230 landowners and one for every 125 000 voters.

The Third Duma lasted five years from 1907, and its members mostly co-operated with the government. The Fourth Duma was elected in 1912, with only property owners being allowed to vote. But the Dumas solved nothing. They had little real power and anyway the Tsar closed them down or fixed the elections to get the result he wanted.

Stolypin

The Tsar did have the sense after 1905 to realise that some changes were necessary if his power were to survive. He sacked Witte and appointed Peter Stolypin as his prime minister.

A The political parties in the four Dumas. Parties of the Left wanted drastic changes, the Liberals and the Conservatives wanted only moderate changes, and the right-wing groups supported the Tsar's government. The 'national minorities' represented non-Russian peoples in the Empire. Although the Social Democrats won some seats in the elections, for most of this period their representatives refused to attend the Duma as a protest against the government.

	First Duma	*Second Duma*	*Third Duma*	*Fourth Duma*
Parties on the Left				
Social Democrats	0	65	14	14
Socialist Revolutionaries (SRs)	0	34	0	0
Trudoviki (allies of the SRs)	94	101	14	10
Liberal parties				
Kadets	179	92	52	57
Progressives	0	0	39	47
Conservatives				
Octobrists	17	32	120	99
Right-wing groups	15	63	145	152
National minorities	120	130	26	21

B Peter Stolypin.

Stolypin was born in 1862 and had been a civil servant and a provincial governor. He was known to be clever and strong-minded. He believed in a 'carrot and stick' approach: making some changes for the better, but also dealing ruthlessly with any signs of disobedience. He realised that it was important to get the peasants on the Tsar's side, to act as a force for stability in the countryside. He therefore passed laws to wipe out the peasants' debts and he made it easier for them to buy their own land. However, relatively few peasants took advantage of this opportunity, preferring the old system by which poorer peasants supported each other through local organisations called village communes. The peasants who did become better off were known as **kulaks**, and they later played an important part in Russian history.

Stolypin improved education in Russia, and improved conditions in the armed forces. He also encouraged the building of more factories but at a pace which would not cause massive overcrowding in the cities. He believed that a strong and prosperous Russia was the best guarantee against people supporting revolution.

Elsewhere Stolypin showed his ruthless streak. Strikers and revolutionaries were tried in special courts all over Russia, and many were executed. In other parts of the Empire he introduced a policy of 'Russification'. This meant that national groups like the Poles, Ukrainians and Finns had restrictions put on the use of their own native

C The cover of an anti-government magazine, published after the 1905 Revolution. The caption reads 'In this world there is a Tsar. He is without pity. HUNGER is his name.'

languages, and they lost other rights.

Stolypin had many enemies, even in the government, and Nicholas II increasingly disliked him because Stolypin thought that the Duma

Between 1906 and 1909 over 3000 people were hanged for taking part in the 1905 Revolution. The gallows became known as 'Stolypin's necktie'.

did have an important part to play in Russia. He was assassinated in 1911 by a police agent. His policies had only limited success, but at least he had tried to save the Tsar's rule.

D Stolypin's views.

[On becoming prime minister in 1906] I must carry through effective measures of reform, and at the same time I must face revolution, resist it and stop it.

[A later quotation] The government puts its faith not on the drunken and the weak but on the sober and the strong.

After Stolypin, Nicholas II was even more isolated and was seemingly unaware of how unpopular he was becoming, even among many better off people who were his traditional supporters.

Rasputin

The Tsar knew little about governing. In 1905 a previously obscure 'holy man' called Rasputin, who had travelled around Russia, arrived at court. He gained favour with the Tsar and Tsarina through his apparent ability, possibly with the aid of hypnosis, to control the dangerous illness of their son. The Tsar and Tsarina became increasingly dependent for advice on Rasputin, or 'Our Friend' as they called him. Later, during the First World War, Rasputin even gave advice on whom the Tsar should appoint to his government.

Rasputin was a colourful character. He had sympathy for ordinary Russians and was intelligent enough to predict disaster if ever Russia got involved again in a major war. But he was also notorious for his orgies and wild living at court, and although the personal conduct of the Tsar and his wife was blameless, their friendship with Rasputin was bad for their own reputation.

F A Russian cartoonist saw Rasputin manipulating the Tsar and his wife like puppets.

E Rasputin surrounded by some of his female admirers at court.

СПРУТЪ

№ 8.

16 февраля 1906 г.

Видъ на землю съ луны.

G The cover of an anti-government magazine. The caption reads 'The view of Earth from the Moon'. The Russian Empire is shown in red.

Rasputin himself said: 'The aristocrats can't get used to the idea that a humble peasant should be welcome at the Imperial Palace ... They are consumed with envy and fury.' He was assassinated in 1916 by a group of aristocratic Russians who disliked his influence over the Tsar and the government.

Russia in 1914

Russia was changing by the time war broke out in 1914. More money was being spent on schools and more children were learning to read and write. More peasants owned their own land. Trade unions had finally been permitted. Some revolutionaries doubted that there would be a revolution in their lifetime. But the number of strikes was also increasing. In 1912 over 200 strikers at the Lena goldfields were massacred by soldiers. Although industrial production was going up, the condition of the industrial workers was getting worse.

Historians still argue about whether Russia was becoming a better place under the Tsar, or whether it was heading for a repeat of the 1905 Revolution. But the First World War was to bring a new set of problems, even more serious than the old ones.

Q

1 a) Why did Nicholas set up the First Duma?
  b) What powers were the Dumas allowed?
  c) How did Nicholas II try to influence the election results?
2 Look at source A.
  a) Which parties were well-represented in the Dumas, and which were less well-represented? How did this change between 1906 and 1914?
  b) How useful are parliamentary election results to an historian who wants to know about people's views at the time?
  c) Why might the results of the Duma elections after the Second Duma be less useful for this purpose?
3 a) What were Stolypin's policies for avoiding another revolution?
  b) How successfully did he carry out the policies he described in source D?

4 a) What impression of Russia at this time is given by sources C and G?
  b) Would the Tsar and Stolypin have agreed with the message of these two pictures? Explain your answer.
5 a) How important was Rasputin to what was going on in Russia?
  b) What do sources E and F suggest about Rasputin and why he was unpopular with many people?

Extended writing
Were the Tsar and his government more secure in 1914 than they had been in 1905? Use the evidence in this chapter and earlier ones in making up your mind. Points to consider include the personality and actions of the Tsar and those of his ministers; the development of the economy; the situation of the Russian people; and the activities of the Dumas.

Lenin and the Bolsheviks

How important was Lenin's early career? What was Marxism–Leninism, and how did Lenin adapt it to Russian conditions?

The making of a revolutionary

Vladimir Ilyich Ulyanov was born in 1870, the son of a school inspector. This made his family quite privileged by Russian standards. Ulyanov had a good education and was to have become a lawyer. However, his elder brother was hanged in 1887 for his part in a plot to kill Tsar Alexander III. The younger brother then became a revolutionary himself and took the name *Lenin*, after a Russian river.

Lenin believed strongly in the ideas of Karl Marx. Marx was a German who spent much of his life in London up to his death in 1883, studying and writing about the industrialised countries of western Europe. He was particularly interested in two groups of people: **capitalists** and the proletariat. Capitalists were people who owned factories, businesses or land. In other words they had *capital*, or wealth. But Marx wrote that it was the proletariat, the workforce in the factories, who really created the wealth. Yet workers were paid low wages, while capitalists took the profits. One day, said Marx, the workers would rebel and take over the factories and the government.

Marx believed that this would lead to socialism, and eventually to Communism. Source A attempts to explain what these two words mean.

Marxism in Russia

Lenin and a few other Russians believed very firmly in these ideas and formed the Social Democratic Party in the 1890s. They did face a particular problem, however. Marx had assumed that a working-class revolution would occur first in a country like Britain or Germany, which had a lot of industry and a large proletariat or working class. Lenin had to adapt Marx's ideas to Russian conditions. He knew that revolution was difficult in a country like Russia, where the government ruled autocratically and used the secret police to seek out and suppress revolutionary groups. Therefore Lenin believed that only a small, secretive, dedicated party could operate effectively and persuade the Russian working class to become revolutionary. The Social Democrats argued bitterly over these tactics, which became known as Marxism–Leninism. Lenin's opponents wanted a larger party that would contain a variety of people and which would operate more openly.

Bolsheviks, Mensheviks and Socialist Revolutionaries

In 1903 Lenin's arguments were accepted at a party conference held in London, and so his followers became known as **Bolsheviks**, the Russian word for 'majority'. His opponents in the party were the **Mensheviks**, or 'minority'.

SOCIALISM

A system in which the state (another word for government) is run in the interests of ordinary people. Factories, railways, mines – perhaps even land – are nationalised. This means that they are taken over by the government and are run for the benefit of the people and not for profit. Citizens are given equal opportunities and there is less of a gap between rich and poor. Some socialists believed this could be achieved peacefully, some believed in revolution

COMMUNISM

A system which goes beyond socialism, in which differences between classes, and classes themselves, would disappear. Eventually even organised government would 'wither' away because no one would need to force people to obey laws. The Russian Bolsheviks changed their name to the Communist Party in 1918. Communists believed in a one-party state and that violent revolution was the way to achieve first socialism and then a Communist classless society

A Socialism and Communism – a brief explanation.

B A Marxist cartoon from 1901. The royal family is shown at the top of a pyramid. Beneath it are businessmen, soldiers, churchmen, and workers at the bottom. The captions, from top to bottom, read 'We rule you' (the workers); 'we mislead you' (the workers); 'we shoot you' (the workers); 'we' (the workers) 'work for you' (the other classes) 'and feed you'.

There were other revolutionary groups. By far the largest were the Socialist Revolutionaries, which put their faith in a peasant revolution. Their membership was much larger than the Bolsheviks, but less well organised.

For a long time the Bolsheviks had little real hope of success. Several of their leaders, Lenin included, spent many years in prison or in exile in the interior of Russia. Lenin and his colleagues also spent several years abroad and were in Switzerland when the First World War broke out. Although the 1905 Revolution had failed, Lenin still regarded it as a valuable practice or 'dress rehearsal' for another attempt. Yet, by 1914, Lenin's dreams of a revolution leading to socialism in Russia seemed as unrealistic as ever.

C Lenin writing in the revolutionary newspaper *Iskra* ('The Spark') in 1900.

Organise for the determined struggle against the autocratic government and against the whole of capitalist society … If we have a strongly organised party, a rebellion in a single area may flare up into a victorious revolution … Before us, in all its strength, towers the fortress of the enemy from which a hail of shells and bullets pours down upon us, mowing down our best warriors. We must capture this fortress.

D From a Communist Party questionnaire, completed by Lenin in 1921 when he had been leader of Russia for over three years:

Date of birth/age: 1870 – 51 years.
State of health: Good.
Family dependants: Wife and sister.
Nationality: Russian.
Native tongue: Russian.
Knowledge of other languages: English; German; French – poor; Italian – very poor.
What part of Russia do you know well and how long have you lived there? Know Volga country where I was born best; lived there until age 17.
Have you been abroad? (when, where, how long): In a number of west European countries – 1895, 1900–05, 1908–17.
Educated: Graduated Petrograd University, Law Faculty, in 1891.
Basic occupation before 1917: Writer
Participation in the revolutionary movement before 1917: Member of the Russian Social-Democratic Workers' Party since its foundation. 1894–5, St Petersburg; 1895–7, prison; 1898–1900, Siberia; 1900–05, abroad; 1905–07, St Petersburg; 1908–17, abroad.
Penalties suffered for revolutionary activities: 1887 prison; 1898–1900 Siberia; 1900 prison.
How long in prison: Several days and 14 months.
How long in exile: Three years.
How long a political refugee: 9–10 years.

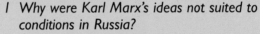

1 Why were Karl Marx's ideas not suited to conditions in Russia?

2 'We must train people who will dedicate themselves to the revolution for not a spare evening but the whole of their lives.' (Lenin in 1900.) How did Lenin adapt Marx's ideas (Marxism–Leninism)?

3 Can you suggest why the 1903 party conference was held in London and not Russia?

4 What were the differences between the Bolsheviks and Mensheviks?

5 What evidence is there in source B that it is a Marxist cartoon? Think about the way in which the workers are being treated.

6 What can you learn from source C about Lenin's character and ideas?

7 Look at source D and other evidence in this chapter. Had Lenin died before 1917, do you think that his career would have been regarded as a failure? Had he achieved any of his aims? If not, what were the reasons?

Russia in the First World War

Why did Russia do so badly in the First World War? Was the Tsar to blame? What effect did the war have on the people of Russia?

'The Russian army is drowning in its own blood.' This dramatic declaration was made by a Russian general, who was in despair at the costly effects of the First World War on his country.

A Russian troops marching through Petrograd at the beginning of the war.

Disaster in the First World War

Russia joined the war in 1914 in alliance with Britain and France against Germany and Austria-Hungary. At the beginning most Russians were patriotic and enthusiastic about the war. Only the Bolsheviks refused to support the war: they believed that it was being fought solely in the interests of the rich people and those ruling Russia, not the workers. But the mood soon changed as the

In 1914 there were 6.5 million men ready to fight in the Russian army, but there were only 4.7 million rifles available.

B A letter from the Tsarina to her husband at the front in 1915.

Never forget you are and must remain autocratic Emperor … Deary, I heard that that horrid Rodzianko [President of the Duma] and others beg the Duma to be at once called together - oh please don't, it's not their business, they want to discuss things not concerning them … Forgive me, but I don't like the choice of the Minister of War … isn't he Our Friend's enemy?

Russian army suffered defeat after defeat, and the casualties mounted up.

Rasputin had warned the Tsar: 'With war will come the end of Russia and yourselves and you will lose to the last man.' Rasputin's prophecies were to come true.

Economic problems

The war was very expensive for the government. As the government printed more money to pay for the war, **inflation** occurred – that is, a rapid rise in prices as money was worth less and less. But the number of workers had risen considerably during the war as the government set up factories and produced more iron, steel and engineering goods. As supplies of food to the towns dried up and prices rose, there were more and more strikes in the factories of Moscow and Petrograd. Meanwhile peasants preferred to sell less of their food since the money they got in exchange was worthless. This made the shortages even worse.

C A queue for bread.

The government under threat

There were many danger signs for the government. Between 1915 and 1917 there were four prime ministers, and other ministers came and went as the Tsarina and Rasputin continually nagged Nicholas II to make changes. Although the Duma gave its support to the Tsar at the start of the war, it grew angry at his refusal to listen to its advice. Rodzianko warned the Tsar that he might force his subjects 'to choose between you and the good of the country'.

Russia would probably not have won the war even if the Tsar had co-operated with the Duma and other well-meaning people in Russia. But his stubbornness certainly did not help the situation.

Meanwhile Lenin and several other leading Bolsheviks were sitting out the war in neutral Switzerland. They condemned the war but could do little except write **propaganda** to be smuggled back into Russia.

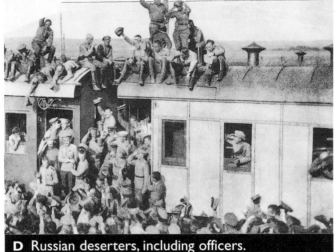

DIE RUSSISCHE ARMEE LÖST SICH VÖLLIG AUF..

D Russian deserters, including officers.

E Reasons for Russia's defeat in the war.

- The German army was better trained, better equipped, and better led than the Russian army. By 1915 the Germans had invaded Russian territory.

- Millions of Russian soldiers died, were wounded, or were captured. Many soldiers deserted and returned to their homes, particularly after the failure of General Brusilov's great offensive in 1916.

- The Tsar became Commander-in-Chief in 1915, but he was no more successful than his other generals.

- With the Tsar at the front, decisions in Petrograd (the new, more Russian-sounding name given to St Petersburg) were increasingly made by the unpopular Rasputin and the Tsarina.

- The war disrupted ordinary life, and there were considerable shortages of food and fuel, especially in Petrograd and Moscow. Russia lacked enough railways and good roads to transport troops and materials.

- There was growing unrest against the government from within the Duma. Rasputin was murdered in 1916 by Russians keen to improve the image of the Tsar. But the murder did not stop people blaming the Tsar.

F Police reports on the situation in Russia in October 1916.

The mass of the population is at present in a very troubled mood … Complaints were openly made about the corruption of the government, the unbelievable burdens of the war, the unbearable conditions of everyday life … People expressed the view, without exception, that 'we are on the eve of great events' in comparison with which '1905 was but a toy' … in the words of other Kadets 'everyone understands that under the old order the Germans cannot be beaten'.

Q

1 Why did the Russian army do badly in the war?
2 In what ways did the war make conditions inside Russia worse? If you can, pick out both economic and political reasons.
3 a) Why did the war make people more dissatisfied with the Tsar, the Tsarina and Rasputin?
   b) How did people show their dissatisfaction?
4 a) Both sources A and D are photographs of Russian soldiers at different times during the war. How do you explain the differences between what the two photographs show?
   b) The caption to source D is German. Explain how this might affect the reliability of the source and the impression it gives.
5 Source F is from a police report. How reliable do you think it is likely to be as evidence for the problems in Russia during the war? Give reasons to explain your answer.
6 How much was the Tsar to blame for Russia's problems in the war? When considering your answer, think about those problems faced by Russia before the war started, and those problems which came about after the war started, or were made worse by it. How much was the Tsar personally to blame for what happened?

The March Revolution

What caused revolution to break out in Russia in March 1917? Why was it successful?

Dates in Russian history can be complicated. Until 1918 the Russians used a calendar which was thirteen days behind that in use in other European countries. Some books refer to the February Revolution of 1917. This book will call it the March Revolution, since that is the modern date for it.

Revolution in Petrograd

Nobody expected a revolution early in 1917, although many people expected some kind of trouble. Russia was in chaos. In Petrograd the temperature was 35 degrees below zero. The largest factory in the city, the Putilov Engineering Works, was closed due to lack of fuel. Hungry and frozen women queued for hours on end to buy basic necessities like bread, which was in short supply in the shops.

Strikes broke out and factory workers poured on to the streets. Women and factory workers rioted. Bakeries were looted. As usual in such situations, police and then soldiers were sent to restore order. Then something strange happened. Soldiers who had previously been loyal to the government now mutinied and refused to fire on the demonstrators. The mutineers included the famous Volynsky Regiment. In desperation, Rodzianko, President of the Duma, telegraphed the Tsar. (See source A.)

At the time of the Revolution, the Bolsheviks were the smallest of the revolutionary parties, with about 25 000 members.

A A message from the President of the Duma to the Tsar, 27 February 1917 (old date).

The situation is serious … The government is paralysed; the transportation system has broken down; the supply systems for food and fuel are completely disorganised. General discontent is on the increase. There is disorderly shooting in the streets; some of the troops are firing at each other. It is necessary that some person enjoying the confidence of the country should be given the job of forming a new government straight away. There can be no delay.

However, the Tsarina's interpretation was different. (See source B.)

B A letter from the Tsarina to Nicholas II, 26 February 1917 (old date).

This is a hooligan movement, young people run about and shout that there is no bread, simply to create excitement, along with workers who prevent others from working. If the weather were very cold they would all probably stay at home. But all this will pass and become calm, if only the Duma will behave itself.

The abdication of the Tsar

Because of the breakdown of law and order, the Duma decided to take over the government, although the Tsar ordered it not to meet. The Tsar did not want to give up power. He wanted to return to the capital to take control, but the railway was blocked. Finally he accepted that he had little support left, and he **abdicated** in a railway carriage at Pskov station. The 300-year-old Tsarist dynasty of the Romanovs was at an end.

C A loyal Russian soldier trying to prevent his comrades deserting.

News of this revolution came as a surprise to Lenin in Switzerland. He immediately made preparations to return home.

Was it a revolution?

The Tsar had gone, but not much else had changed. Was it really a revolution? A British newspaper reporter writing in May 1917 thought that between four and five thousand people had been killed in Petrograd, but that: 'In the provinces the revolution was of a paper character, being carried out mainly in the telegraph offices. Normal life was scarcely interrupted for more than one day in Moscow, and even less in other cities.'

What had changed? Later there were many different interpretations of how the March Revolution had come about, as the following sources show.

D From a child's textbook written in Communist Russia in 1976:

In response to the call of the Bolsheviks the workers of Petrograd factories went on strike … The Bolshevik Committee met late at night in a small house on the outskirts. 'We can no longer wait and do nothing. The time has come to act openly. We shall begin tomorrow. We must seize the arms stores and disarm the police,' the Committee decided.

E A report by a member of the secret police who had infiltrated the Bolshevik Party.

The movement which has started has flared up without any party preparing it and without any discussion first of a plan of action. The revolutionary circles began to react only toward the end of the second day when the desire to develop the success of the movement to the widest limits possible became noticeable … The movement started spontaneously, without any preparation, due entirely to the food crisis.

F Demonstrators outside the Tsar's Winter Palace during the March Revolution.

G A statement from Zenzinov, the President of the Socialist Revolutionaries.

The revolution fell like thunder out of the sky. Let us be frank; it arrived joyfully unexpectedly for us revolutionaries too.

Could the Tsar have survived? In 1917 there were divisions between the working classes and the upper classes, as there always had been. But now many people in the upper and middle classes who had traditionally supported the Tsar no longer had any faith in him. If Nicholas II had been able to keep these people on his side, then order might have been restored without a change of government. But the Tsar lacked the skill or willingness to act in a way which would reassure his old supporters. Therefore although he alone was not responsible for Russia's problems, there were few people in Petrograd sorry to see him go in 1917. Trotsky wrote: 'The dynasty fell by shaking, like rotten fruit.'

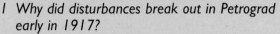

1 Why did disturbances break out in Petrograd early in 1917?
2 Look at source A. Why did Rodzianko urge the Tsar to change the government?
3 Look at source B. Compare the Tsarina's view of the disturbances with Rodzianko's. Who was right?
4 How is the interpretation in source D different from that of source E? What reasons can you give for this difference?
5 Why did the Tsar finally abdicate?
6 Historians often divide the causes of major events like revolutions into long-term and short-term causes. Make two lists, one for long-term and one for short-term causes of the March Revolution, and place the causes below in the correct list. If you can think of any further causes not given here, add those also.

Defeats in the First World War; the activities of revolutionary groups; the disloyalty of some troops; shortages of food and other essential things; failure of the government to give land to the peasants; the activities of Rasputin; dissatisfaction within the Duma; the character of the Tsar; memories of the 1905 Revolution; Russia's backwardness; poverty.

Russia Between Revolutions, March–November 1917

How was Russia governed between March and November 1917? How successful was the Provisional Government in dealing with Russia's problems?

The Provisional Government and the Soviet

After the Tsar's abdication, someone had to run the country. Members of the Duma formed themselves into a Provisional Government. Nobody had elected this government, and therefore it was called 'provisional', meaning it was a temporary arrangement until elections could be held for another parliament. However, the elections were postponed, because the war was still going on.

The Provisional Government did not intend to sweep away everything from the past. Nevertheless there were some important changes. Political prisoners were freed, including many Bolsheviks. Newspapers could now print what they liked. Revolutionary exiles were allowed to return home.

There was another important development. During the March Revolution the Petrograd Soviet, which had first appeared in 1905, was again formed. Unlike the Provisional Government, the Petrograd Soviet was elected by workers, soldiers and sailors. It included several revolutionaries who wanted to change things much more drastically. It issued its own orders to workers and soldiers. The Soviet also issued Order Number One, stating that it would obey the government only if the Soviet thought it was running Russia in the right way. This apparent sharing of power between the Provisional Government and the Petrograd Soviet is often known as 'dual government'.

Many of the Bolsheviks were prepared to support the Provisional Government because they believed that Russia was not yet ready for a socialist revolution. Most Marxists believed that the events of March meant the middle class was taking power from the Tsar. They expected that there would then be a long period during which the working class would become better organised, and then Russia would take part in a genuine world-wide revolution in which the proletariat or workers would set up their own state.

Kerensky

Alexander Kerensky, a socialist member of the Petrograd Soviet, was also Minister of Justice in the Provisional Government. He soon became Minister of War and then Prime Minister. Opinions about Kerensky varied, as sources A and B suggest.

A Bruce Lockhart writing about Kerensky in *Memoirs of a British Agent* (1932):

> He was an honest, if not a great man. Sincere, in spite of his oratorical talents [his ability to make inspiring speeches], and, for a man who for four months was worshipped as a god, comparatively modest.

B From the diary of Louis de Robien, a French diplomat in Petrograd:

> Kerensky is in reality nothing but an inspired fanatic, a nutcase and a madman. He acts through intuition [guesswork] and personal ambition, without reasoning and without weighing up his actions.

Many people were very enthusiastic about the Provisional Government at first. Some Mensheviks and Socialist Revolutionaries even became government ministers. But the enthusiasm did not last long. The government soon ran into serious difficulties. Some were of its own making, and some were caused by circumstances beyond its control.

Kerensky wanted to continue fighting the war against the Germans. He hoped that victories would strengthen his own position and that of the government. But a Russian offensive against the Germans in the summer of 1917 failed. All the problems described in earlier chapters also continued: shortages, desertions and casualties.

Under Lenin's leadership, the Bolsheviks were the only revolutionary party which refused to allow any of its members to join the Provisional Government.

C A poster produced to persuade Russians to lend money to the government for the war.

D A demonstration in Petrograd, July 1917.

E A description of conditions in Petrograd in September and October 1917 by the American journalist John Reed.

Week by week food became scarcer. The daily allowance of bread fell from a pound and a half [675 grams] to a pound, then three-quarters, half, and a quarter-pound. Towards the end there was a week without any bread at all … For milk and bread and sugar and tobacco one had to stand in queues for long hours in the chill rain. Coming home from an all-night meeting I have seen the queues beginning to form before dawn, mostly women, some with babies in their arms.

Lenin's return to Russia

Lenin had returned to Russia in April. The German government arranged a special train to take him from exile in Switzerland to Petrograd, via Sweden and Finland. The Germans knew that Lenin wanted to stop the war, and they thought that if Lenin caused trouble in Russia, it would disrupt the Russian war effort against Germany.

On his arrival at the Finland Station in Petrograd, Lenin caused some surprise, even to his own followers. He read out the *April Theses*, which was his programme for the Bolsheviks.

F Lenin's *April Theses* included the following points:

- **The Provisional Government must be overthrown.**
- **The war must be ended immediately.**
- **Industry must be nationalised.**
- **Land should be given to the peasants.**
- **All power must be given to the soviets.**

Lenin's programme was summed up in the words 'Peace, Bread and Land' and 'All power to the soviets'. These were effective slogans in 1917.

G A Soviet painting showing Lenin addressing a crowd. How does this painting show Lenin in a favourable way?

The July Days

At first things were difficult for Lenin. He had to persuade his colleagues that he was right. Then in July there were mass demonstrations in Petrograd against the war. Lenin was reluctant to join in, knowing that the Bolsheviks were not yet strong enough to seize power. However, he was persuaded to give his support to the demonstrations, known as the 'July Days'. When Kerensky's government managed to suppress the demonstrations, Lenin was forced to flee in disguise across the Finnish border in order to avoid arrest. Other Bolshevik leaders were arrested. Rumours spread that Lenin was being paid as a spy by the Germans.

The Kornilov revolt

Events now started to go Lenin's way. The new commander of the Russian army, General Kornilov, distrusted Kerensky's ability to fight the Germans. He also wanted to destroy the Petrograd Soviet, which was calling for peace. Kornilov wanted to set up a military dictatorship, and when his troops approached Petrograd, Kerensky was forced to rely upon Bolshevik armed 'Red Guards' to block the advance. The Bolsheviks persuaded many of Kornilov's men to desert.

H The July Days. The police open fire on demonstrators in Petrograd.

I Lenin's false identity card, showing him beardless and in disguise. He used this card when avoiding arrest in 1917.

J A photograph of Kerensky taken whilst he was Prime Minister in 1917.

would not get the support they needed, and they even leaked news of the meeting to the newspapers. However, Kerensky's government, increasingly isolated, took few effective steps to protect itself.

Lenin was determined to go ahead. Trotsky had only joined the Bolsheviks in the summer of 1917, but he was given the task of organising the actual seizure of power. Detailed preparations were made.

Kornilov's rebellion collapsed and the Bolsheviks boosted their image as 'Defenders of the Revolution'. In contrast, Kerensky's government was seen as increasingly weak. In the countryside peasants were seizing land for themselves. Military discipline was breaking down as more and more soldiers deserted – 'voting with their feet' as Lenin put it.

The Bolsheviks decide

Only Lenin of all the party leaders appeared to have clear, confident aims. He was now claiming that he wished to seize power not just for the Bolsheviks, but in the name of all those represented in the soviets. At the end of August and the beginning of September the Bolsheviks won majorities in the Moscow and Petrograd Soviets for the first time.

Lenin still had to persuade the other leading Bolsheviks that the time was right to seize power. He returned secretly from Finland to attend a meeting of the Central Committee of the Bolshevik Party. The Committee voted 10–2 in favour of carrying out a second revolution by seizing power in the name of the workers and the soviets. The two who disagreed were Zinoviev and Kamenev. They were afraid that the Bolsheviks

Q

1 What steps did the Provisional Government take to win support after the Tsar's abdication?
2 What was the Petrograd Soviet, and what was 'dual government'?
3 What impression of Kerensky is given by sources A and B? What problems do these two sources cause for an historian writing about Kerensky?
4 What was revolutionary about the April Theses?
5 Do sources C and D prove that the Provisional Government was well supported in its first few months? Explain your answer.
6 Source H is a frame from a feature film about the Russian Revolution made ten years later. The film, made in Communist Russia, made the July Days seem like a very dramatic affair. But a British historian described the events of July as 'a very small setback for the Bolsheviks'. How could there be two such different interpretations?
7 What effect did the Kornilov revolt have on the Provisional Government and the Bolsheviks?
8 Study source E and other evidence in this chapter. Did the Provisional Government succeed in solving the problems caused by the war? If not, why not?

The November Revolution

Why was there a second revolution in Russia in 1917? How important was the role of Lenin and the Bolsheviks in bringing it about?

Lenin and Trotsky prepare

'The Great October Socialist Revolution' was the grand Communist title for what turned out to be quite a small-scale affair, although the results were to be very important for Russia and the world for years to come. This revolution took place in October according to the old calendar. It is other-wise known as the November Revolution.

On the eve of the November Revolution Lenin returned from Finland for good. He came to the Smolny Institute in Petrograd, the Bolshevik head-quarters. Although Lenin was in charge, it was Trotsky who had done most of the planning.

The plan was for the Bolsheviks to strike at the same time as the All-Russian Congress of Soviets was meeting in Petrograd. This organisation repre-sented all the revolutionary parties, not just the Bolsheviks. The Bolsheviks knew that the Mensheviks and some other members of the Congress would oppose their method of seizing power.

Source A shows some of the most important buildings and bridges in Petrograd. The armed Bolshevik Red Guards were sent to seize them. They had already won over some of the troops in the Petrograd garrison and in the Peter and Paul Fortress. The cruiser *Aurora*, with a Bolshevik crew, was to sail up the River Neva and fire its guns as a signal for the Red Guards to capture their targets.

The Bolsheviks strike

Although Kerensky had a good idea of what was planned and had closed down the Bolshevik news-paper offices, he did not have enough loyal troops to protect his government. The Red Guards took control of the capital. There was little fighting, much less than in March. The Bolsheviks did have to capture the Winter Palace but they achieved this relatively easily, and arrested the members of the Provisional Government who were meeting there.

The All-Russian Congress of Soviets was also meeting while these dramatic events were unfolding. When they discovered what was happening, the Mensheviks and most of the Socialist

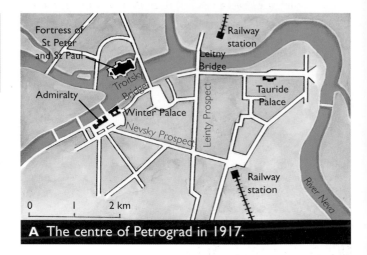

A The centre of Petrograd in 1917.

Revolutionaries walked out of the meeting in protest at the Bolsheviks having taken the law into their own hands, without their agreement. Trotsky shouted after them: 'You are pitiful, isolated indi-viduals. You are bankrupts, your role is played out. Go where you belong from now on … on to the rubbish heap of history.' By walking out, the other revolutionary parties left the Bolsheviks in control.

B Trotsky describes the Bolshevik headquarters in his autobiography *My Life* (1930).

> On the third floor of the Smolny, in a small corner room, the Committee was in continuous session. All the reports about the movement of troops, the attitude of soldiers and workers, the agitation in the barracks … the happenings in the Winter Palace – all these came to this centre.
>
> All that week I had hardly stepped outside of the Smolny; I spent the nights on a leather couch without undressing, sleeping in snatches, and constantly being roused by couriers, scouts, messenger-cyclists, telegraphists, and ceaseless telephone calls.

C Stalin praises Trotsky's role in the revolution in *The Role of the Most Eminent Party Leaders* 6 November 1918.

> All the work of practical organisation of the insurrec-tion was conducted under the immediate leadership of the Chairman of the Petrograd Soviet, Trotsky. It is possible to declare with certainty that the swift passing of the garrison to the side of the Soviet and the bold execution of the work of the Military Revolutionary Committee [the group of Bolsheviks organising the Revolution], the Party owes principally and above all to comrade Trotsky.

D Y Kukushkin, a Soviet historian, describes the assault on the Winter Palace in *History of the USSR* (1981).

The signal for the start of the assault was given from the cruiser *Aurora* which fired a blank shot from her bow gun … the formations of Red Guards, sailors and soldiers poured out of the adjacent streets and street corners in an irresistible rush across the square in front of the Winter Palace … The last bastion of counter-revolution [forces opposed to the Revolution] fell on the night of October 25–26, 1917. This marked the victory of the armed uprising of the working people in the capital of Russia, Petrograd, which [began] a new era in human history.

E A scene from the Soviet film *October*, made in 1927 to celebrate the tenth anniversary of the October/November Revolution.

F John Reed describes what happened inside the Winter Palace in *Ten Days That Shook the World* (1966).

Carried along by the eager wave of men we were swept into the right-hand entrance, opening into a great bare vaulted room, the cellar of the east wing, from which issued a maze of corridors and staircases. A number of huge packing-cases stood about, and upon these the Red Guards and soldiers fell furiously, battering them open with the butts of their rifles, and pulling out carpets, curtains, linen, porcelain, plates, glassware … The looting was just beginning when somebody cried, 'Comrades! Don't take anything. This is the property of the People!' Immediately twenty voices were crying, 'Stop! Put everything back! Don't take anything! Property of the People!'

The ministers of the Provisional Government were arrested in the Winter Palace, apart from Kerensky, who managed to flee abroad. The following day Lenin drew up a decree which declared that power had been taken over by the Congress in the name of the soviets of all Russia.

G Soldiers and civilians demonstrating in the streets of Petrograd during the November Revolution.

Why did the Bolsheviks win?

The Bolsheviks had not won because they were an irresistible force. Far from it. They won because Kerensky and the Provisional Government had lost respect and support, other political parties were hesitating, and only Lenin appeared to offer decisive leadership. Therefore a relatively small group, the Bolsheviks, was able to seize control of the capital. A few days later they also seized control of Moscow. They now controlled the two largest cities, but little else. The real struggle was about to begin.

Q

1 How important was Trotsky's part in the November Revolution?
2 Use source A and other information in the chapter to describe the part played in the November Revolution by the Red Guards.
3 Why was there opposition to the Bolshevik Revolution from within the All-Russian Congress of Soviets?
4 What evidence of propaganda is there in sources D, E and F? What impression do these sources give of the events of the November Revolution? What was the intention of the people who produced these sources?
5 How was Lenin able to seize power with only a relatively small party?

Extended writing
Why was there a second revolution in Russia in 1917 so soon after the first? There are several points you might consider in answering this question, including: the continuation of the war; the role of Lenin and the Bolsheviks; the weaknesses and problems of the Provisional Government. Were all these things, and others, equally important in bringing about revolution?

The New Soviet State

How did the Bolsheviks alter life inside Russia? What was the Bolshevik system of government like?

The Bolshevik success in November 1917 came as a surprise to almost everyone, and few believed that Lenin would succeed in staying in power. None of his supporters had any experience of governing. They had to work out what to do whilst fighting opponents at home and from abroad.

Peace with Germany

The first need was for peace. The Germans had invaded Russia and were threatening Petrograd. A cease-fire, or armistice, was arranged with them. Trotsky was sent off to negotiate with the Germans, and eventually the Treaty of Brest-Litovsk was signed in March 1918. The terms of the peace were very harsh, and Trotsky was forced to give up large areas of the old Russian Empire. Lenin persuaded his colleagues that they had no choice; otherwise the Germans would destroy his government. Anyway, Lenin was confident that world revolution was about to break out elsewhere, including Germany, in which case the treaty would not last long.

Russia lost:

26% of its population
27% of its arable land
26% of its railway mileage
74% of its iron ore and coal

During the Civil War the Communists regained some of the lost territories

FINLAND

Petrograd
ESTONIA

•Moscow
RUSSIA

LATVIA
Baltic Sea
LITHUANIA

PART OF
POLAND BYELO-
RUSSIA

Ukraine

Black Sea Georgia

····· Russia's 1914 border

Territory lost at Brest-Litovsk which the Russians did not regain in the Civil War

Territory lost at Brest-Litovsk which the Russians did regain in the Civil War

A Territory lost by Russia at the Treaty of Brest-Litovsk.

The Constituent Assembly

Back in Petrograd, meanwhile, many changes were underway. The Provisional Government had always intended to hold elections for a new parliament, called a Constituent Assembly. This would give all Russians the chance to vote for their future. But the elections had been postponed because of the war. Now the Bolsheviks allowed the elections to take place. The results are shown in source B.

As soon as the Assembly met, Lenin had it closed down. He declared it 'counter-revolutionary'. He had no intention of giving up power.

Bolsheviks	175 deputies
Socialist Revolutionaries	370 deputies
Left Socialist Revolutionaries (allies of the Bolsheviks)	40 deputies
Mensheviks	16 deputies
Kadets	17 deputies

B The results of elections to the Constituent Assembly.

A new Russia

Many laws were passed to change Russia:

- businesses and trade were nationalised;
- peasants were allowed to take over the land;
- women were given equal rights to men;
- the Church had its wealth taken by the government;
- different peoples in the old Russian Empire were given the right to be independent.

A new system of government was created. Instead of having government ministers as in Britain, there were **commissars** appointed to take charge of foreign affairs, industry and so on. In Britain the most important government ministers form the Cabinet, which helps the prime minister to govern. The equivalent in Russia was the Council of Peoples' Commissars, called SOVNARKOM for short. But in 1919 the Politburo was created. It contained a few leading Bolsheviks such as Lenin, Trotsky and Stalin. It met every week and made important decisions. Another organisation, called the Orgburo (Organisational Bureau), was responsible for carrying out decisions made by the Politburo. It was assisted by the Secretariat. Joseph Stalin was the only Bolshevik to belong to the Politburo, Orgburo and Secretariat. This was important in helping him come to power, as will be explained in a later chapter.

One-party rule

Other political parties such as the Mensheviks, the Socialist Revolutionaries and the Kadets were quickly weakened by the arrest of their leaders and the closing down of their newspapers. By 1921 Russia was already a 'one-party state'. That party was the Communist Party, the name adopted by the Bolsheviks in 1918. The secret police or Cheka was set up to arrest real or imagined opponents of the Communists.

In theory, decisions were still made by the Central Committee of the Communist Party. This was elected by an annual meeting or congress of important Party members. But since it met much less frequently than the Politburo, the Central Committee could not make day-to-day decisions.

Only about five per cent of the population became Party members. To become one, you had to be recommended by two existing members, and then serve a probationary year to show how suitable you were. A Party member was expected to do things like explain Communist propaganda to workmates, and behave like a good citizen. A relatively small number of Communists became full-time Party workers. There was also a Party youth movement called the **Komsomol**.

D 'The People of the whole World welcome the Red Army of Labour' – a Communist poster.

E 'Red Moscow is the Heart of the World Revolution' – another Communist poster.

There were other organisations in the new state. There were elected local soviets, but their powers were quickly reduced. From 1923, all citizens could vote for the Supreme Soviet, but there was only one candidate in each **constituency**, and the Supreme Soviet was less important than the Party.

This system sounds complicated, but it is important to understand that the Soviet Union was run in this way until the late 1980s. The key fact is that, whoever was in the government, *real* power lay with the Communist Party, and its leader, the General Secretary.

Q

1 a) How harsh were the terms of the Treaty of Brest-Litovsk for Russia?
   b) Why did Lenin and Trotsky sign the Treaty?
2 Look at source B.
   a) Explain whether the Bolsheviks would have been satisfied with the result of the elections to the Constituent Assembly.
   b) Why did Lenin close the Assembly down?
3 Did the Communists bring about more changes in Russia than the Provisional Government had done? Explain your answer.
4 What is meant by a 'one-party state'?
5 a) What was the intended message of source C?
   b) What reasons did workers and peasants have to be pleased about the Bolsheviks' success in winning power?
6 a) What view of the Russian Revolution is put across in sources D and E? Who were the posters probably aimed at?
   b) What would have been the likely attitude of governments in other countries to these posters? Why would a non-Communist's view of these events be likely to have been different from that of a Bolshevik?

C A Communist poster soon after the Revolution.

Civil War and Foreign Intervention, 1918–21

Why did Civil War break out in Russia in 1918? Why did foreign countries become involved in the Civil War? Why were the Bolsheviks or Reds able to win the Civil War? What effect did the Civil War have on Russia?

Opposition to the Bolsheviks

The Communists had won power mainly because their opponents had been weak and poorly led. Once Lenin's enemies began to organise themselves, the Bolshevik government faced a serious threat to its survival. Opponents saw no reason why they should obey the Communists. Communists were not well known and had not been elected, but rather they had seized power by force.

One of the earliest Communist decrees or laws allowed all the subject peoples of the old Russian Empire to have their independence from Russia. The Communists were too weak in any case to stop them. There were movements to break away in Finland, in the Baltic region, and in the Caucasus region to the south. The Ukrainians set up their own parliament, made a separate peace treaty with the Germans, and soon began fighting the Communists.

Meanwhile, in the south of Russia, several army officers loyal to the old regime formed anti-Communist armies. Admiral Kolchak and Generals Denikin and Wrangel became leaders of the so-called White armies. Their followers and supporters were not just soldiers but came from many different groups. They included businessmen, landowners, and others who had suffered from Lenin's takeover by losing their land and businesses.

After the Constituent Assembly was closed down, other left-wing or revolutionary parties also sought to overthrow the Communists. Even their former allies, the Left Socialist Revolutionaries, split with the Communists over the Treaty of Brest-Litovsk and the way in which the Communists attacked the richer peasants. The SR leader Chernov formed a Socialist Revolutionary government in the Volga region, and another SR government was set up in Archangel in the north.

Everywhere the Communists were under threat. Even Lenin himself was shot and wounded by Dora Kaplan, a Socialist Revolutionary.

Foreign intervention

The Communists, or Reds, as they were known, were further threatened when other countries began to interfere in Russia in the first half of 1918. 17 foreign governments, including the British, American, French and Japanese sent armies for several reasons. These governments were angry that the Communists had made peace with the Germans. They wanted to see a non-Communist Russian government in power that would restart the war against Germany and take the pressure off their troops in western Europe. They were also hostile to Lenin's government because it refused to pay the Tsar's debts to foreign countries and had nationalised foreign-owned industries. Foreign governments also knew that the Communists preached world revolution, and so they wanted to get rid of the Communists before they could cause trouble elsewhere.

British troops landed at Murmansk in the north, and with the Japanese at Vladivostock in the far east.

A 'Have you volunteered yet?' A Bolshevik recruiting poster for the Red Army.

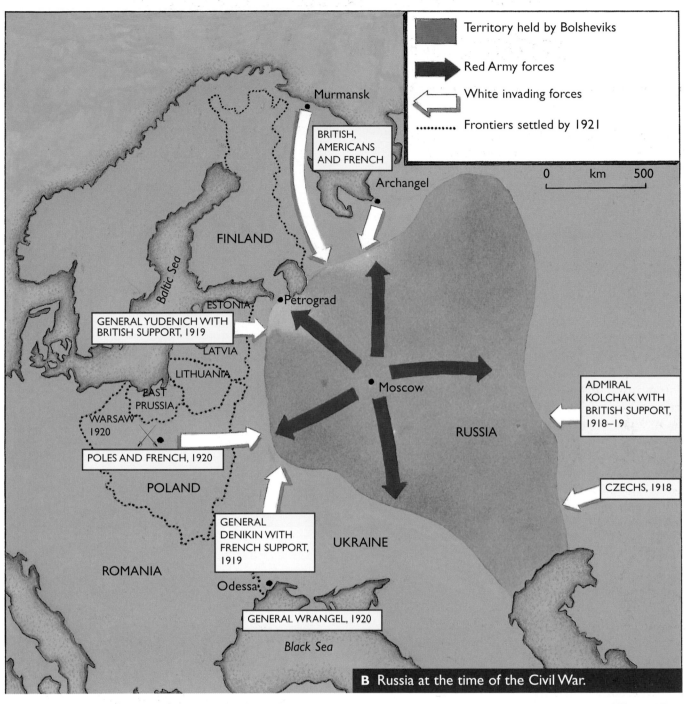

B Russia at the time of the Civil War.

Legend:
- Territory held by Bolsheviks
- Red Army forces
- White invading forces
- .... Frontiers settled by 1921

0 km 500

Map labels:
- Murmansk
- BRITISH, AMERICANS AND FRENCH
- Archangel
- FINLAND
- Baltic Sea
- ESTONIA
- Petrograd
- GENERAL YUDENICH WITH BRITISH SUPPORT, 1919
- LATVIA
- LITHUANIA
- EAST PRUSSIA
- WARSAW 1920
- POLES AND FRENCH, 1920
- POLAND
- Moscow
- RUSSIA
- ADMIRAL KOLCHAK WITH BRITISH SUPPORT, 1918–19
- CZECHS, 1918
- GENERAL DENIKIN WITH FRENCH SUPPORT, 1919
- UKRAINE
- ROMANIA
- Odessa
- GENERAL WRANGEL, 1920
- Black Sea

British and French troops landed in the south. The Germans themselves occupied the Ukraine and west Russia. A large army called the Czech Legion also joined the anti-Communist crusade: this was a unit formed from Czechs who had been captured during the First World War and had agreed to fight on the Russian side against their Austrian masters. They too wanted Russia back in the war. The Czech Legion took control of the Trans-Siberian railway. Both Moscow and Petrograd were soon under threat. Source B shows how the Reds were surrounded by enemy armies.

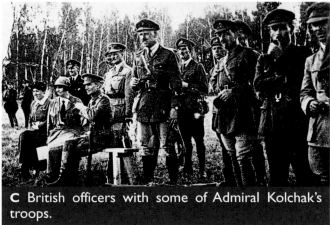

C British officers with some of Admiral Kolchak's troops.

The Bolsheviks turn the tide

Lenin was aware of the danger to the Reds, but he was also optimistic.

D Lenin speaking in November 1918.

> **Our position has never been so dangerous as now … The imperialists of the Anglo-French-American group are thinking of building a Chinese wall, to protect themselves from Bolshevism, like a quarantine against plague … The germ will pass through the wall and infect the workers of all countries.**

Although the position of the Reds looked hopeless, they actually had several advantages over their opponents. The Reds fought desperately, knowing that if they lost, they would certainly be killed. Trotsky formed a new army, the Red Army, and turned it into a feared fighting force. When there were not enough officers, he **conscripted** former Tsarist officers into the army. Discipline was ruthless. In contrast, the foreign armies were already exhausted by several years of world war, and could not be expected to fight with the same determination in a foreign country.

Many peasants did not like the Reds. But at least Lenin had given them their land. They feared that if the White generals won the war, Tsarism or something like it might be restored to Russia. Therefore they either tried to keep out of the war or supported the Reds.

E A Bolshevik propaganda poster representing France, America and Britain as evil capitalists trying to control Russia.

F Bodies of Reds killed by Whites during the Civil War.

Finally, the Reds controlled most of the railways and the large towns of Russia. They managed to move their troops quickly to where they were needed. They were united, whereas the Whites and foreign armies fought mostly as separate groups.

The end of the war

Most of the fighting was over by 1920. Kolchak was captured and executed by the Reds. The other White generals retreated and the foreign armies left Russia.

The last stage of the war involved a struggle against the new country of Poland. The Poles wanted to extend their territory eastward, and invaded the Ukraine in 1920. The Reds managed to drive them back almost to Warsaw, and then themselves were defeated and forced back. Peace was made between Russia and Poland at the Treaty of Riga in 1921.

The effects of the war

All wars are brutal, and civil wars particularly so. Atrocities were carried out on both sides. Prisoners were often tortured and killed. Instead of recovering from the effects of the First World War, Russia suffered three more years of devastation during the Civil War.

The Tsar and his family had been kept prisoner by the Reds in Siberia and then at Ekaterinburg in the Urals. In July 1918 Kolchak's White army was approaching the town, and the Reds were afraid that the Tsar might fall into White hands. The Red guards herded the royal family into a cellar, shot them all, and burned their bodies in a nearby mine.

During the Civil War Lenin and Trotsky ran Russia ruthlessly. They tolerated no opposition, and the local soviets or councils lost most of their powers. Decisions were made by the people running the Communist Party.

Although the Reds won the Civil War, they did not forget how close they had come to defeat by foreign armies. For years afterwards the Soviet government remained suspicious of the motives of foreign governments, and many Communists believed that they would only be safe if they helped bring about revolutions in other countries.

> In order to enforce discipline and discourage desertion from the Red Army, Trotsky ordered one man in every ten in some regiments to be shot.

G A proclamation by Whites in July 1918.

The Soviet of People's Commissars has brought ruin to Russia … Instead of bread and peace it has brought famine and war. The Soviet has made of mighty Russia a bit of earth dripping with the blood of peaceful citizens doomed to the pangs of hunger … The People's Commissars are arresting and shooting workers who do not agree with their policies, are manipulating the elections, and are strangling all freedoms.

During the Civil War, the Communists set up an organisation called the Communist International, or Comintern. Its task was to help set up Communist parties in other countries and to work for an international Communist revolution. This helped to increase suspicion of Communist Russia among foreign governments.

There were 0.5 million Communists serving in the new Red Army during the Civil War. Most people who joined the Communist Party did so after the Revolution and so their early years in the Party were dominated by fighting. These new Party members were not prepared to put up with any opposition and in the years ahead were often prepared to use force to get their way.

However, the Communists were keen to end their isolation. Soon after the end of the War, in 1922, they signed the Treaty of Rapallo with Germany, another country defeated in the First World War. Soon afterwards other countries, including Britain, agreed to recognise officially the Communists as the legal government of Russia, although they remained suspicious of 'the Reds'.

Q

1 a) Who were the Bolsheviks' enemies inside Russia in 1918?
  b) Why did they fight the Reds?
2 Why did foreign governments join in the Civil War?
3 Why were the Tsar and his family killed?
4 Why did the Reds win the Civil War? Was it due to their own strengths or the weaknesses of their enemies?
5 a) What do sources E, F and G tell us about the nature of the Civil War?
  b) Which of sources E and G best explains the differences between the Whites and the Reds?

War Communism

What was War Communism? Why was it introduced? How did it affect Russia and its people?

The new Russia

The Bolsheviks hoped to create a new society in Russia after the revolution. They wanted a country in which the old **ruling class** and wealthy people lost their money, land and businesses. They believed that the country should be run for the benefit of ordinary people. However, Lenin faced several difficulties in trying to achieve this.

- Many people in Russia still opposed the Bolsheviks or were only interested in their own affairs.
- Russia was already a backward country. Now it had been further devastated by several years of war.
- Between 1918 and 1920 the Bolsheviks had to devote most of their energies to fighting the Civil War.

Changes in the economy

Despite these problems, the Communist Party made a start on taking over the economy. A decree or law passed soon after the revolution nationalised the factories. This means that the government took many of them from their previous owners. Other factories were taken over and run by ordinary workers themselves.

It was soon discovered that there were not enough experts and experienced managers to go round, and so the Communists had to co-operate with some of those who had been in positions of responsibility before the revolution. These people belonged to the class to which Lenin often referred as the **bourgeoisie**, or middle class.

This did not seem like the socialism or Communism that Marxists had expected. Not much had changed in the economy except that now the government claimed to be running things in the interests of ordinary people.

Lenin set up an organisation called the 'Supreme Council of National Economy' to make plans for the future. But there was a severe shortage of food and other basic goods in Russia. So prices rose rapidly and money soon became worthless. Some Communists, like Nicholas Bukharin, liked this inflation. They hoped that

money would disappear, since in a Communist society people would work for each other and be given what they needed. But during this time people had to barter, or exchange food and goods, since their money had no value.

War Communism is introduced

The policy of the government from mid-1918 to 1921 was known as War Communism. War Communism was not one particular law or decree, but a whole series of measures designed to take control over everyone's lives.

The most urgent need was for food, particularly in the towns. The peasants wanted to keep the land which they had just been given. But they were also unwilling to sell the food they grew. Why should they when money was worthless and there was nothing to buy in exchange? So Lenin ordered squads of soldiers and Party officials to go into the villages and **requisition** food – that is, seize it without payment.

> Because of shortages in the towns, almost half the inhabitants of many Russian cities left them between 1918 and 1920 and went to live in the countryside.

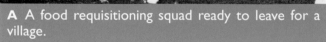

A A food requisitioning squad ready to leave for a village.

The peasants were very unhappy at this. Sometimes they attacked the requisition squads. Sometimes they themselves were shot. Less food was grown. By 1921 only half the amount produced before the First World War was grown, even in areas like the Ukraine, which had the best farmland.

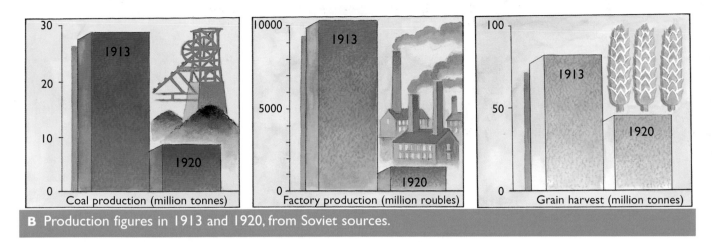

B Production figures in 1913 and 1920, from Soviet sources.

There was famine, and it is estimated that over seven million Russians died of hunger or disease during the period of War Communism. In 1921 even the Communist newspaper *Pravda* admitted that one Russian in every five was starving.

Industry also had its problems, as source B shows. It was decreed in June 1918 that all industry was to be nationalised. Russians were conscripted to work in factories. But most effort went into producing materials for the army, which was fighting the Civil War.

C Starving peasants buying and selling human flesh during the famine.

Opposition

Not surprisingly, many ordinary people rebelled against the harshness of War Communism. Workers in factories worked more slowly, or went on strike. Even more serious for Lenin, there was opposition from within the Communist Party. One group, called the Workers' Opposition, argued that War Communism was wrong and that the Communists should do more for the working class.

The situation was critical. The police were shooting strikers, and trade unions were banned. There was a real danger that if ordinary people turned against the Communists, they would be overthrown.

Lenin had already made the decision to abandon War Communism before the explosive events at Kronstadt in 1921 (see pages 30–31) showed just how unstable the situation was.

Q

1. What changes did the Communists make to (i) agriculture and (ii) industry in the period of War Communism, 1918–21?
2. Why did (i) most peasants and (ii) some Communists oppose War Communism?
3. a) What does source B tell us about the effects of War Communism?
   b) These figures are official figures collected by the Soviet government. Does this mean that they are likely to be reliable as historical evidence?
4. Did the experience of War Communism prove that the Communists could not run Russia successfully? Consider carefully what had happened in Russia both before 1917 and between 1918 and 1921 before you answer this question.

Key Issues

How important was the Kronstadt Revolt? Why was 1921 an important year for the development of Communism in Russia?

The Kronstadt Rebellion

During 1920 and 1921 there were several rebellions against the harshness of Communist rule in Russia. In March 1921 the most serious of these broke out in the naval base of Kronstadt, an island just outside Petrograd. Thousands of sailors protested against their living conditions and what had been happening in Russia. They disliked the way in which the Communist Party did not appear to have much regard for ordinary people, and had taken away the powers of the local councils or soviets. The sailors demanded a 'free socialist democracy'.

A The manifesto of the Kronstadt rebels.

We joined the Communist Party to work for the good of the people and stand for the help of the workers and peasants. The worker, instead of becoming master of the factory, became a slave ... Those who dare to say the truth are imprisoned to suffer the torture cells of the Cheka [secret police] or are shot.

The sailors of Kronstadt had helped the Bolsheviks seize power in 1917, and they had fought for them during the Civil War. Therefore their rebellion against Lenin seemed particularly serious.

The rebellion had to be crushed. Trotsky sent the Red Army across the iced-up sea to attack the naval base. In a three-week struggle many of the rebel sailors were killed, and later thousands were imprisoned or executed. It was the last occasion in Soviet history that there was a large-scale organised rebellion against Communist rule.

C Trotsky reviewing Red Army troops in 1920.

D From the diary of Alexander Berkman, a supporter of the rebels, in 1921:

One by one the embers of hope have died out. Terror and despotism have crushed the life born in October ... Dictatorship is trampling the masses under foot. The Revolution is dead; its spirit cries in the wilderness ... The Bolshevik myth must be destroyed. I have decided to leave Russia.

B Red Army soldiers crossing the ice to attack Kronstadt.

The Tenth Party Congress

As described in the previous chapter, Lenin had already decided that War Communism had to be abandoned. The Kronstadt Rebellion simply convinced him further.

The Communist Party held yearly meetings or congresses in order to discuss policy and elect officials. The Tenth Party Congress of March 1921 was one of the most important in Russian history, for two reasons. Firstly, Lenin talked about the need for unity in the Communist Party. Secondly, he announced the end of War Communism. It was to be replaced by the New Economic Policy, which is described in the next chapter.

A ban on arguments

Many members of the party were feeling optimistic at the Congress, because the Civil War was virtually over. The Whites had been defeated and foreign troops had left Russia. But there were many arguments going on inside the Party. Apart from the Workers' Opposition mentioned in Chapter 11, there was a group called the Left Communists. These included Bukharin. They believed that in order for Communism to survive and develop in Russia, the Party should help to start workers' revolutions in other countries, to get foreign allies. Another group was the Democratic Centralists, who believed that ordinary Party members should have a bigger say in how decisions were made and carried out.

Lenin was worried that **factions** within the Party would weaken it and encourage opponents. Therefore at the same time as announcing changes to the economy, the Tenth Party Congress also issued a declaration on 'party unity'. In future, anyone in the Party who openly disagreed with the official policy would be 'purged'. In the early 1920s this meant being sacked from the Party.

The one-party state

Lenin's decisions had important results. They meant that in future any Communist who disagreed with the Party's way of doing things risked being labelled as a traitor to the leadership. This gave great power to those already high up in the Party like Joseph Stalin, who could silence opposition by claiming that he was carrying out Lenin's wishes.

There were still some Mensheviks and Socialist Revolutionaries active in Russia in 1921. But now they were silenced, arrested or shot by the secret police. The Communist Party gradually increased its hold over the way people thought and acted. Schoolchildren were taught only the Communist point of view. Thousands of churches were closed down and had their property taken by the government. The Communists said that religion was something used by capitalist governments to keep people oppressed and in ignorance. There was **censorship**, which meant that newspapers, books and films were only allowed if they carried the 'right' messages. Russia was rapidly becoming a totalitarian society – a country in which the ruling Party controlled not only what people did, but even what they thought.

E Communists destroying a monastery.

Q

1 Why did the Kronstadt Rebellion break out?
2 a) In what ways does source D support source A in its attitude towards the Communist government?
   b) What did the author of source D mean by 'the embers of hope have died out' and 'the Revolution is dead'?
3 What is meant by a one-party state or a totalitarian state? Do these descriptions fit Russia after 1921?
4 Why were the Kronstadt Rebellion and the Tenth Party Congress both important events in the history of Communist Russia?

The New Economic Policy

What was New Economic Policy? What were its successes and failures? Why did it cause controversy?

Changes to the economy

Lenin announced the New Economic Policy, or NEP, at the Tenth Party Congress of 1921. It made two important changes to the way in which the Soviet economy was organised.

First, in agriculture, the government stopped the practice of requisitioning food, that is, forcibly taking it from the peasants. Peasants now had to supply a fixed amount of what they grew to the government. Any extra they were allowed to keep or even sell for a profit.

Second, in industry, small factories (those employing less than 20 workers) were **privatised**. This means that the government returned them to private ownership. However, all important industries, such as coal and steel, the transport system and foreign trade, remained nationalised. Lenin called these 'the commanding heights of the economy' and believed that they must be controlled by the government for the benefit of everyone.

A new rouble was brought in, in order to help end inflation. The programme of electrification continued, and it was extended to rural areas. Lenin said: 'Soviets plus electrification equals communism.' In other words, communism was not just an idea, but brought real progress to the Russians.

A Russian peasants in 1923.

The impact of NEP

After 1921 the improvements in the economy were rapid. The Civil War was over and people felt more secure. Peasants now realised that it was in their interest to produce as much food as possible, and make a profit. Between 1921 and 1927 the amount of cultivated land grew by 50 per cent.

In the towns workers produced more and there was more to buy. It was now legal to trade and make a profit, so many Russians began to make a living out of buying and selling, rather than actually making things. As a result, a new class of traders called 'Nepmen' grew up.

Russia soon recovered from the terrible experiences of War Communism. However, not all economic problems were solved. In the early years of NEP the price of food fell as more was produced. But the output of industrial goods could not keep pace: because there were still shortages, the prices of industrial goods rose, and some peasants could not afford to buy things. The government was worried that the peasants might start producing less food again.

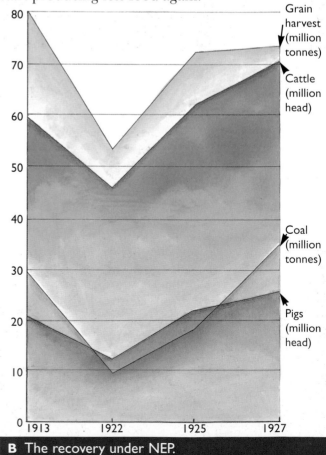

B The recovery under NEP.

Worries about NEP

Some members of the Communist Party had more serious worries about NEP. To them it seemed like a backward step. They thought that by allowing private ownership, private trade and profits, Lenin was bringing back capitalism. Class differences were reappearing as some people made profits. In the countryside, some peasants became rich from selling their produce, and even began to employ poorer peasants to work for them. These richer peasants were called kulaks.

In the towns, Party members began to complain at the appearance of Nepmen, who made a living by trading rather than making things. Some said that NEP encouraged greed and selfishness, with people trying to make money for themselves rather than work for the good of everyone. Communism seemed further away than ever.

Lenin admitted in 1921 that NEP was a 'retreat'. He said that, had War Communism not been abandoned, the Communist government would have been overthrown by the people. But he also said that NEP was a temporary measure, a sort of 'state capitalism'. The important thing was to strengthen Russia and make it easier for Russia to become socialist in the future. Lenin stated that it was important that workers and peasants should co-operate with each other.

Nobody was prepared to challenge Lenin. However, after his death, leading people in the party argued more and more about whether NEP should be continued. There were two main worries:

- Could Russia ever be a socialist country whilst NEP encouraged a minority to become rich at the expense of the majority?

- Could Russia go on risking a situation in which the government and people living in towns depended on the goodwill of the peasants to produce enough food? The Communist Party had relatively few members in the countryside. Would the peasants hold the Communists to ransom, and stop the party introducing proper socialism?

All the worries and the arguments became mixed up with quarrels about who would become leader of Russia after Lenin's death in 1924. It was to be the opponents of NEP who eventually won the day.

C A speech by Lenin to Communist Party members in 1921.

We are retreating, going back as it were, but we are doing this so as to retreat first and then run and leap forward more vigorously. We retreated on this one condition alone when we introduced our New Economic Policy … so as to begin a more determined offensive after the retreat.

D Victor Serge, a former Communist, regretted what happened under NEP (*From Lenin to Stalin*, 1937).

In a few years' time the NEP restored to Russia an aspect of prosperity. But to many of us this prosperity was sometimes distasteful…we felt ourselves sinking into the mire [bog or swamp] – paralysed, corrupted … There was gambling, drunkenness, and all the old filth of former times … Classes were reborn under our very eyes … There was a growing gap between the prosperity of the few and the misery of the many.

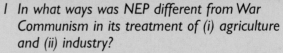

E A Soviet cartoon from 1927, making fun of Nepmen.

Q

1 In what ways was NEP different from War Communism in its treatment of (i) agriculture and (ii) industry?
2 Look at source B. In what ways and to what extent did the economy improve under NEP?
3 Look at source C. How did Lenin justify bringing in NEP?
4 Look at source D and the other evidence in this chapter. Why were many Communists unhappy about what happened under NEP?

Extended writing
'NEP changed Russia for the better.'
Using your own knowledge, and the evidence in this chapter, explain whether you agree or disagree with this interpretation.

Lenin

How important was Lenin to the success of Communism in the USSR?

Lenin did not enjoy good health for long. He survived an assassination attempt by a Socialist Revolutionary in 1918, but in 1922 he suffered his first stroke. Although he continued as leader he was severely disabled and finally died in January 1924. He was 54 years old. At his funeral millions came to pay their respects. His body was embalmed in a tomb in Moscow's Red Square. Petrograd was renamed Leningrad in his memory.

A Building the mausoleum for Lenin's body.

Lenin had devoted all his adult life to first trying to bring about a revolution in Russia and then keeping the Communists in power. He disliked all the attention and near-worship that he received after 1917, but without his leadership the Communists would probably have not won power. In the difficult years before 1914 it was Lenin who had fiercely argued for a determined, disciplined Bolshevik Party, dedicated to revolution. When he returned to Russia in April 1917, it was Lenin who persuaded the Bolsheviks not to co-operate with the Provisional Government. He took advantage of the confusion and uncertainty to lead a second revolution.

After 1917 Lenin acted ruthlessly when he thought it necessary, to keep the Communists in power. Although Trotsky was a great speech-maker and led the Red Army to victory in the Civil War, it was Lenin alone who had the respect of all the other leading Communists.

Nobody challenged Lenin's leadership. However, towards the end of his life he did worry a great deal about what was happening in Russia and who would succeed him as leader.

Lenin was actually responsible for some of the things he claimed to dislike. For example, during his time in power the Communist Party became more rigid in its views, and ordinary members lost the chance to have a real say in making decisions. The Party was dominated by the Central Committee. In 1919 Lenin created the 'People's Commissariat of State Control', used to keep Party members in line. He put Stalin in charge of this organisation, and then came to regret it. All opposition outside the Party was crushed by the feared Cheka or secret police. Lenin personally justified the use of terror against opponents.

B From a Soviet school textbook published in 1976:

On January 21, 1924 Lenin died. Millions of people were overcome with sorrow … On the morning of January 27 his remains were brought to Red Square, where an endless mass of people streamed past the coffin. The working people of the entire world also paid their last tribute. Factory workers in many countries stopped work for five minutes in homage … For the first time in the history of mankind the death of one man moved hundreds of millions of people throughout the world. Everyone had heard the name of Lenin.

ТОВ. Ленин ОЧИЩАЕТ

C A pro-Bolshevik cartoon about Lenin from 1917. It is called 'Sweeping the Earth of Evil Spirits'.

D The crowd at Lenin's funeral.

E From *The Times* 23 January 1924:

This extraordinary figure was first and foremost a professional revolutionary … A man of iron will and inflexible ambition he had no scruple about methods and treated human beings as mere material for his purpose. Short and sturdy, with a bald head, small beard and deep-set eyes, Lenin looked like a small tradesman. When he spoke at meetings his ill-fitting suit, his crooked tie … turned the crowd in his favour … This is not the place to describe in detail the terrible achievements of Bolshevism – the shameful peace with Germany, the plundering of the educated and propertied classes, the long continued terror with its thousands of innocent victims … The Communist experiment brought Russia to economic ruin, famine and barbarism.

F A photograph from the 1980s, showing Communist Young Pioneers in Moscow's Lenin Museum.

Nevertheless, when Lenin died, there was genuine grief not just among Russians but among millions of people around the world who regarded him as the champion of oppressed people. Sources B to F show some of the opinions of Lenin and the propaganda about him.

G From a Soviet poem called 'By Lenin's Study', written in 1956 by Alexander Yashin:

Since dawn he'd stood there at attention,
Unnoticed.
Down the corridor bright, As Lenin worked
They brought him endless
Communications, wires and letters, and comrades came to talk with Lenin –
The soldier knew them all by sight
The frontline news was serious.
Lenin
Met peasants, like a friendly host
He saw them to the door
Where always
The soldier waited at his post.
Then Lenin, noticing the soldier,
A spare chair in his study found.
He held the door with one foot open
And said:
'Dear fellow, please sit down!'
Well, what's so special? Lenin got him
The chair, was thoughtful, took some pains …
That sums up Lenin! And explains
Why this has never been forgotten.

Q

1 Look at sources B, C, D and G. What messages about Lenin do these sources try to give?
2 Does source E give a different impression of Lenin? Does the fact that it comes from a British newspaper make it less useful to an historian?
3 Look at source F. Why did young Communists hold their ceremonies in the Lenin Museum?
4 Can propaganda be useful to an historian? Use these sources in your answer.
5 Make a list of five ways in which Lenin improved Russia, and five ways in which he did not. Then answer this question: 'How important was Lenin to the success of Communism in Russia?'
6 Source E claims that Lenin brought Russia to 'ruin, famine and barbarism', whereas source B claims that hundreds of millions were saddened by Lenin's death. How do you explain this difference in interpretation? (Think carefully about the origins of these sources.)

The Rise of Stalin

How did Stalin succeed in becoming leader of the Soviet Union?

Early years

Joseph Stalin was born to a poor family in Georgia in 1879. He was educated in a religious college, but was expelled for revolutionary activities. He was soon an active member of the Bolshevik Party. He organised bank raids to get money for the party, and spent some time in Tsarist prisons.

Stalin was in Russia at the time of the March Revolution in 1917, and was editor of the Bolshevik newspaper *Pravda*. But he was not as well known as Lenin or Trotsky.

General Secretary

After the November Revolution Stalin was promoted by Lenin. He was good at organising and getting things done. In 1922 Lenin made him General Secretary of the Communist Party. This made Stalin very powerful, since he knew all the details of party members' lives. He could also promote his own loyal followers.

Stalin distrusted Leon Trotsky. Trotsky was clever and a great speechmaker. He helped to organise the November Revolution. He also created and led the Red Army during the Civil War. However, he had much less support among ordinary Party members. He first quarrelled with Stalin during the Civil War, but dismissed him as a 'mediocrity' (a person of little ability).

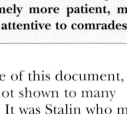

A Members of the Soviet Politburo in 1924 – Stalin is at the top and, from left to right, are Zinoviev, Trotsky, Kamenev, Bukharin, Rykov and Tomsky.

As Lenin's health declined he grew worried about Stalin, who had a reputation for ignoring people's feelings. In 1922 Stalin upset Lenin by his rough treatment of Georgians who were seeking independence from Russia. Lenin wrote his 'Testament' or will, in which he made clear his doubts about either Stalin or Trotsky following him as leader. (See source B.)

B From Lenin's Testament, 1923:

Comrade Stalin, having become General Secretary, has concentrated enormous power in his hands; and I am not sure that he always knows how to use that power with sufficient caution … I propose to the comrades to find a way to remove Stalin from his position and to appoint to it another man who in all respects is different from Stalin – namely more patient, more loyal, more polite and more attentive to comrades.

Stalin knew of the existence of this document, but fortunately for him it was not shown to many people after Lenin's death. It was Stalin who made the arrangements for Lenin's funeral. Trotsky was not in Moscow. Stalin began to act as if he was the man to continue Lenin's ideas.

Stalin and the opposition

Even before Lenin's death Stalin had made an alliance with Zinoviev and Kamenev, two other leading Communists, to keep Trotsky out of power. After Lenin's death Trotsky, Zinoviev and Kamenev formed the 'Left Opposition'. There was also a 'Right Opposition' group led by Bukharin, Rykov and Tomsky. Stalin presented himself as a moderate man, in the centre of politics. But all the time he was promoting his followers within the Party.

There were many arguments about the path Russia (re-named the Soviet Union in 1924) should follow. Trotsky favoured 'permanent revolution'. He wanted the government to concentrate on spreading revolution to other countries. In contrast, Stalin favoured 'socialism in one country'. This meant that Russia should concentrate on building up its own strength. Trotsky also favoured harsh treatment of the peasants. Stalin allied himself with Bukharin and the Right. In 1927 Trotsky, Zinoviev and Kamenev were defeated and expelled from the Party. By 1929 Trotsky had been expelled from Russia.

Bukharin wanted moderate treatment of the peasants. But having defeated Trotsky, Stalin turned on Bukharin. Bukharin, Tomsky and Rykov were expelled from the government in 1929. Stalin was left in control, virtually as a dictator. He was free to carry out his own policies for agriculture and industry.

Nobody now dared criticise Stalin. In 1924 and 1925 many Party members had been 'purged' or sacked. They had been replaced by the 'Lenin enrolment', Party members who supported Stalin's ideas of transforming NEP Russia into socialist Russia by their own efforts.

Stalin's opponents had failed to prevent his rise to power. They had underestimated him, thinking him not very clever. They also did not have the support which Stalin had within the Party – they argued and changed alliances amongst themselves. But after 1929 there was no question about who had followed on from Lenin as leader of the Soviet Union.

E In this cartoon, Trotsky is accused of sabotaging Stalin's achievements in the USSR.

The end of Trotsky

Trotsky spent the 1930s in exile in foreign countries, eventually settling in Mexico. He continued to campaign against Stalin, claiming that he had destroyed the true spirit of the Russian Revolution and was simply a dictator concerned with his own power. Stalin replied with anti-Trotsky propaganda as shown in source E.

Stalin also had secret agents on Trotsky's trail. In 1940 one eventually found him, and assassinated him by smashing his skull with an ice-pick.

D After Trotsky's defeat, Stalin had all references to him removed. Above is a photograph of Lenin making a speech in Moscow in 1920. It was later altered to remove Trotsky (see the photograph on the right).

Q

1 Why was the post of General Secretary important?
2 Look at source B. Why did Lenin regret having appointed Stalin?
3 What were the Left and Right Opposition and what did they stand for?
4 How was Stalin able to overcome his opponents?
5 Look at source C.
  a) What opinion did Trotsky have of Stalin?
  b) How reliable is Trotsky's opinion likely to be as evidence about Stalin?
6 a) What do sources D and E tell us about Stalin's attitude towards opponents?
  b) Why might an historian find sources D and E useful as evidence about Stalin?

Collectivisation

What was collectivisation? Why was it carried out in the Soviet Union? What were the results?

All Communists believed that socialism could only come about in a modern industrialised country. They believed the Soviet Union must build factories and heavy industry, particularly if they wanted to prevent attack by hostile capitalist states.

However, the Soviet Union in the 1920s was still basically a poor country of peasants. They had been given their land in 1917, because the Communists had not been strong enough to prevent it even if they had wanted. Most Communists disliked private land ownership. They believed that, although many peasants were becoming better off under NEP, they were only interested in themselves. Also the Communist Party had relatively few members in the countryside.

If the Communists of the 1920s were going to industrialise the USSR they would have to work out where the money and workers were going to come from and decide what role the peasants would play in this.

During the struggle for the leadership in the 1920s, two main views were put forward. The Left believed that the peasants should be heavily taxed, and the money used to pay for industrialisation. The Right, led by Bukharin, believed that the kulaks or richer peasants should be encouraged to grow even more. By becoming richer, they would be able to buy more goods and so industry would grow anyway.

B From a speech by Stalin to party members in 1929:

We must break down the resistance of the kulaks and deprive this class of its existence. We must eliminate the kulaks as a class. We must smash the kulaks … we must strike at the kulaks so hard as to prevent them rising to their feet again. We must annihilate them as a social class.

The 'Urals–Siberian method'

The situation became serious in 1927. Peasants were unwilling to sell extra grain, because they wanted higher prices. The government was afraid that there would not be enough food for workers

A A propaganda photograph from 1931 showing Russian peasants enthusiastically queuing up to join a collective farm.

in the towns. In 1928 there was rationing of bread. The government was forced to requisition grain from the peasants as in the days of War Communism. Because of the area in which this happened, this seizure of grain was called the 'Urals–Siberian method'.

The collectivisation programme

Stalin strongly supported this. He was determined that never again should peasants be in a position to threaten Russia's food supplies. Stalin and his followers decided that the answer was to get more control over the peasants and to make farming more efficient. This would also mean that fewer farmers would be needed, and more people would be available to work in industry.

By 1929 the programme of collectivisation had begun. The idea was that in selected areas, the peasants would be persuaded to join their small farms together into large farms called collectives (the Russian word for a collective farm was a *kolkhoz*).

These farms were very large, often covering the area of entire villages. They were either run directly by the government, or more often by the peasants themselves, but managed by a Communist Party member. Members of the collective had one duty above all others: they had to provide a fixed amount of food to the government, which then sold it in the towns. The collective farm workers could share out what was left after all debts were paid.

Many of the poorer peasants were happy to join collective farms. After all, they had little or nothing to lose. The problem came with kulaks. The Party encouraged poorer peasants to attack kulaks and seize their property and belongings. Stalin claimed that while the kulaks existed, there would be no equality in the USSR.

Resistance

The kulaks objected to collectivisation. They attacked Communist Party officials. They burned their crops and killed their animals rather than hand them over to the Communists. Food production fell. Millions of kulaks were imprisoned, sent to remote Siberia, shot, or sent to work in new factories.

The process of collectivisation took several years to complete. In 1930 there was so much opposition that Stalin called a temporary halt to the programme. He blamed over-keen officials, who had become 'dizzy with success'. But the drive to collectivise soon began again.

The results of collectivisation

In 1929 Stalin said 'Can the kulak be allowed to join the collective farm? Of course not! He is the accursed enemy of collectivisation.'

By the mid 1930s most of the USSR's farmland was collectivised. What were the results?

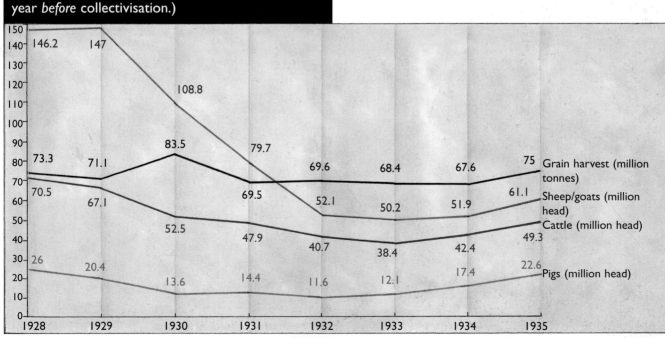

C The results of collectivisation, from Soviet sources. (*Note:* the figures for 1928 are for the last year *before* collectivisation.)

Grain harvest (million tonnes)
Sheep/goats (million head)
Cattle (million head)
Pigs (million head)

Sheep/goats: 146.2, 147, 108.8, 79.7, 69.6, 68.4, 67.6, 75
Grain harvest: 73.3, 71.1, 83.5, 69.5, 52.1, 50.2, 51.9, 61.1
Cattle: 70.5, 67.1, 52.5, 47.9, 40.7, 38.4, 42.4, 49.3
Pigs: 26, 20.4, 13.6, 14.4, 11.6, 12.1, 17.4, 22.6

1928 1929 1930 1931 1932 1933 1934 1935

Life on the collective farm was not all bad. Some collectives even had schools and hospitals for the workers. They were allowed small plots of private land on which they could grow a few crops or keep animals for their own use. Not surprisingly, peasants usually put more effort into these plots than the collective farm. MTS or Motor Tractor Stations were also built: collective farms could hire tractors from them instead of using the old primitive farming methods.

By 1936 25 million small peasant farms had been replaced by 250 000 collective farms.

D Some peasants' reactions to collectivisation (quoted in *From Lenin to Stalin* by Victor Serge, 1937).

Eighty peasants in this hole-in-the-ground came to the public prosecutor to complain that they had been forced by violence to join the *kolkhoz*. Presidents of *kolkhozes* have been assassinated nearby ... About 15 per cent of the farmers are firmly for the *kolkhozes*. These are the young Communists ... The other peasants go into the *kolkhozes* because they cannot do otherwise, but they make sure to enter with empty hands ... A nearby soviet has just announced the expulsion of 20 poor peasants, some of whom are sincerely devoted to the regime. All are condemned as 'agents of the *kulaks*'. Their crime is that they have not always kept silent, that they have said their condition has grown worse.

E Russian peasants greet the first tractor in their village.

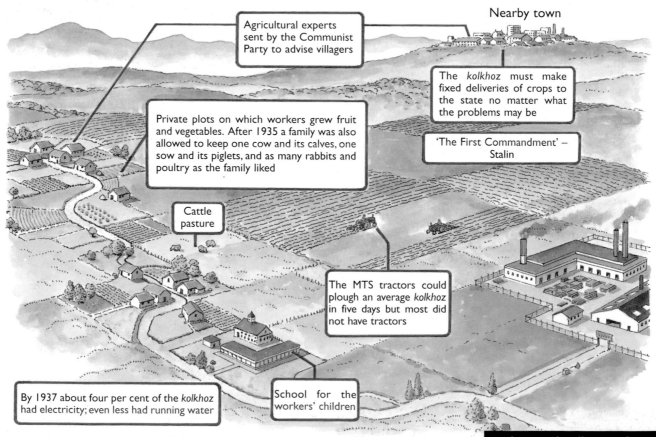

Nearby town

Agricultural experts sent by the Communist Party to advise villagers

The *kolkhoz* must make fixed deliveries of crops to the state no matter what the problems may be

'The First Commandment' – Stalin

Private plots on which workers grew fruit and vegetables. After 1935 a family was also allowed to keep one cow and its calves, one sow and its piglets, and as many rabbits and poultry as the family liked

Cattle pasture

The MTS tractors could plough an average *kolkhoz* in five days but most did not have tractors

By 1937 about four per cent of the *kolkhoz* had electricity; even less had running water

School for the workers' children

F A typical collective farm.

However, the results of collectivisation were disastrous. Over ten million peasants were deported or killed. It took years to recover from the drop in food production. Famine broke out in some areas like the Ukraine, and millions died of starvation. Farming remained inefficient. Soviet farmers produced much less per head than farmers in America or western Europe.

Success at a price

In some ways collectivisation was a success for Stalin and the Communists. They had finally got control of the countryside. The peasants never again openly rebelled against Communist rule. Stalin had also made sure that he had a secure supply of food for the towns, and workers for the factories. This was very important to Stalin. His main aim was to build up industry and to do this, he had to guarantee the food supply for millions of townspeople.

After collectivisation about 35 per cent of the harvest was taken by the government. The government resold grain at four times the price it paid the collective farmers.

There was still not enough food, and some had to be bought from abroad. But, by the middle of the 1930s, there was just about enough for everybody. For Stalin that was all that mattered. He was a brutal ruler, and he was prepared to cause millions of deaths and great unhappiness to achieve what he wanted.

H Stalin on a collective farm.

G A Soviet cartoon showing a peasant working on his private plot rather than on the collective farm.

1 a) Why did many Communists want to change the system of farming in the 1920s?
   b) How did the Right and the Left believe that the peasants should be treated?
2 What was the 'Urals–Siberian method'?
3 Look at source B. How would you describe Stalin's attitude towards the kulaks?
4 What was collectivisation, and why did Stalin favour it?
5 Who resisted collectivisation, and what forms did this resistance take?
6 a) In what ways are sources A, G and H propaganda?
   b) Why did the government feel the need to issue such propaganda?
   c) From what you have read in this chapter, how accurate was the view of collectivisation given in sources A and G?
7 In what ways do sources C and D show the results of collectivisation?
8 Use the evidence in this chapter to decide (i) whether collectivisation was necessary and (ii) whether or not it was a complete disaster for the Soviet Union.

Industrialisation and the Five-year Plans

What was the purpose of the Five-year Plans? How was industrialisation carried out? How successful was it? What effects did it have on the Soviet Union?

During the 1920s Stalin had wanted the USSR to follow a policy of 'socialism in one country'. He meant that the Soviet Union should concentrate on building up its strength by developing much more industry. This would mean building new towns and modern factories, improving transport and communications, and carrying out great industrial projects. The New Economic Policy (NEP) was to be abandoned, and the government would direct the whole programme.

The USSR became the first planned economy in the modern world. This meant that the state, or government, planned exactly what should be made, and where and when it should be made.

The First Five-year Plan

Although some projects were begun in 1927, the First Five-year Plan was officially started in 1928. GOSPLAN, the state planning authority, set targets for every industry, and allocated resources. The targets set were very ambitious, expecting production to be doubled within five years in many industries.

A A propaganda painting showing Stalin urging workers to produce more.

B A propaganda poster before the First Five-year Plan reads 'Industrialisation – the Path to Socialism'.

C From a speech by Stalin in February 1931:

It is sometimes asked whether it is not possible to slow down the tempo somewhat, to put a check on the movement. No, comrades, it is not possible! The tempo must not be reduced! ... To slacken the tempo would mean falling behind. And those who fall behind get beaten. No, we refuse to be beaten ...

We are 50 or 100 years behind the advanced countries. We must make good this distance in ten years. Either we do it, or we shall be crushed.

These targets had to be adjusted. Even so, Stalin declared in 1932 that the Plan had been successfully completed ahead of schedule. Soviet statistics cannot always be trusted to be completely accurate. Nevertheless the results certainly seemed impressive, as source E shows.

	1927–28	1932		1937
Coal (million tonnes)	35.4	64.3		128.0
Oil (million tonnes)	11.7	21.4		28.5
Pig-iron (million tonnes)	3.3	6.2		14.5
Steel (million tonnes)	4.0	5.9		17.7
Electricity (thousand million kilowatt hours)	5.0	17.0		36.2

E Results of the First and Second Five-year Plans.

Enormous efforts had to be made to meet the targets. Thousands of peasants helped to build dams and factories, and to work in them. Millions more people went to work in the growing towns.

Young Communist volunteers worked on some projects. Millions of prisoners in the notorious *gulags* (labour camps) were also put to work. The face of the USSR changed. Typical were the new industrial towns such as Magnitogorsk, built in difficult and remote areas like Siberia.

D A poster from 1931 says that if more nurseries, laundries and canteens are provided, women will be able to contribute to industrial growth.

F Sverdlovsk in the Ural Mountains, in 1928 (top) and then in 1933 (bottom).

43

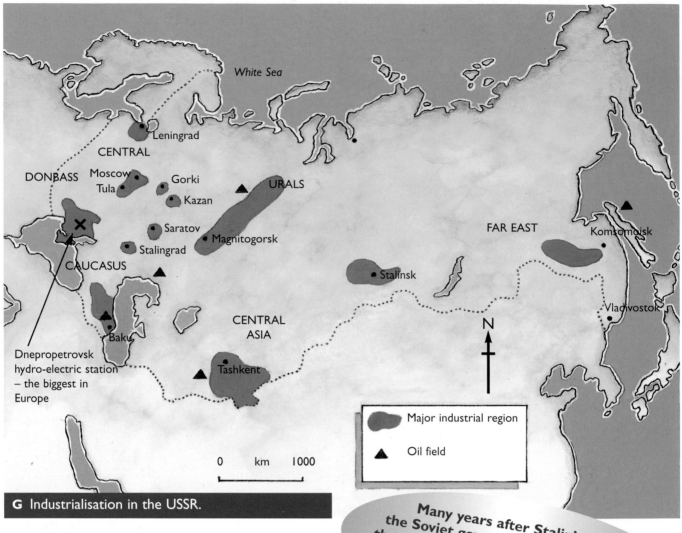

G Industrialisation in the USSR.

Map labels: White Sea, Leningrad, CENTRAL, DONBASS, Moscow, Tula, Gorki, Kazan, URALS, Saratov, Magnitogorsk, Stalingrad, CAUCASUS, Baku, Dnepropetrovsk hydro-electric station – the biggest in Europe, CENTRAL ASIA, Tashkent, Stalinsk, FAR EAST, Komsomolsk, Vladivostok, N

Legend: Major industrial region, Oil field

Scale: 0 km 1000

Working for Mother Russia

Ordinary Soviet citizens found work very hard. Factory discipline was extremely harsh. Those who stayed away from work could be executed. Workers needed permission to change jobs. Factory managers and workers who failed to meet targets were liable to disappear into labour camps. People were under pressure and often frightened.

The government also used propaganda to urge workers to work harder and persuade them that life was getting better, despite all the sacrifices. Good workers were given medals and higher pay. Some workers came from abroad. It was claimed that Alexei Stakhanov had set a world record for the amount of coal mined in one shift, 102 tonnes, which was 14 times the usual amount. Workers who achieved great feats were called 'Stakhanovites'.

Life was also hard because most of the effort of the Five-year Plan went into producing what we call capital or producers' goods. These are things like coal, cement, steel and machine tools. These products are necessary to build up industry,

Many years after Stalin's death the Soviet government finally admitted that Stakhanov had never set a record for mining, and that the whole affair had been a propaganda exercise.

although they are not things that ordinary people need. There was a shortage of consumer goods – things like clothes, radios, furniture – that people wanted to buy in the shops. But workers were told that they had to make sacrifices for a better future.

What was produced was often of a poor quality. Factory managers were only interested in meeting targets for the amount produced, not whether the products were of good quality or not. The quality also suffered because much of the new workforce was unskilled or poorly trained.

Unlike western Europe, there was no unemployment in the USSR in the 1930s. There was a shortage of workers. Millions of Russian women became full-time factory workers for the first time.

H Convicts building the Belomor Canal in the 1930s.

The Second and Third Five-year Plans

The Second Five-year Plan ran from 1933 to 1938. It showed more concern with improving efficiency and quality. It also gave more attention to consumer goods. The Third Plan, begun in 1938, gave more attention to producing weapons, because of the growing threat of war. It was brought to a halt by the German invasion of Russia in 1941.

A new Russia

In the space of little over ten years from 1928, the USSR was changed from a largely agricultural country to one whose power was based on industry. The USSR avoided the Great Depression which badly affected western countries. There was no unemployment, rather a shortage of workers. But the workforce worked hard, and there was little to buy. Later Soviet politicians said that these sacrifices were worth it, because they made it possible for the USSR to survive the terrible coming war with Germany. For Stalin, if the aim was right, any means to achieve it were acceptable.

I From a Soviet school textbook published in 1976:

The Soviet people achieved so much in such a short time because all the country's wealth belongs to the working people who create this wealth … The Stakhanovite movement, as it was called, spread all over the country. Thousands of workers and collective farmers, among them engine-driver Maxim Krivonos, the Vinogradov sisters Maria and Yevdokia who were both weavers, the collective-farm girl Maria Demchenko and the girl tractor-driver Pasha Angelina, topped quotas over and over. This was because they worked for themselves, for their own state. Miracles were created by the free work of the Soviet people.

Q

1 What did Stalin mean by 'socialism in one country'?
2 How did the Five-year Plans organise industry?
3 Look at source C. What reasons did Stalin give for wanting rapid industrialisation?
4 Look at sources D, E and F. Do these sources suggest that the Five-year Plans were successful? Explain your answer.
5 How were workers' lives affected by the industrialisation programme?
6 Stalin claimed that the aim of modernising the USSR and protecting it against invasion justified the use of harsh discipline and temporary suffering. Do you agree?

18

Stalin's Terror

What were the purges and the Terror?
Why did Stalin carry out the Terror?
What impact did it have in the USSR?

Violence and fear had often been part of Soviet life since 1917. After the revolution there had been the killings and the atrocities of the Civil War. After the Civil War members of other political parties were imprisoned or killed by the Communists as Russia became a one-party state. The Soviet secret police, far more efficient than the Tsarist secret police, were constantly rounding up real or suspected opponents of the Soviet system. However, things had become more relaxed for ordinary people as conditions improved under NEP in the 1920s.

The early purges

After 1921 there was a ban on factions within the Communist Party. A faction was a group of Communist Party members who disagreed with the official policy. Arguments continued of course, but Party members who stepped out of line were often 'purged'. This meant that they were sacked from the Party, and lost the privileges which went with membership.

After Stalin came to power at the end of the 1920s, the word 'purge' took on a new and more frightening meaning. It could now mean not just dismissal from the Party, but imprisonment or death, as Stalin was determined to enforce his own way of doing things.

As early as 1928 15 mining engineers at Shakty were executed after being put on trial, accused of sabotaging or wrecking the First Five-year Plan.

The start of the Terror

What became known as Stalin's Terror really began in 1934. That year, at a Congress of leading Party members, Sergei Kirov showed himself to be very popular. He was head of the Communist Party organisation in Leningrad (the city formerly called Petrograd). It was rumoured that many in the Party wanted Kirov to replace Stalin as leader. Later that year Kirov was assassinated at his headquarters. His assassin was killed, but there was a strong suspicion that Stalin had arranged Kirov's murder in order to get rid of a younger rival.

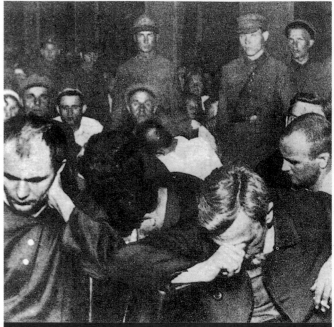

A Victims of the purges hear the death sentence at a trial in 1930.

B Stalin carrying Kirov's coffin at his funeral.

Show trials and mass murder

Whatever the truth, Kirov's murder was used by Stalin as an excuse to begin more extreme purges. Many people, both within and outside the party and including both well-known and ordinary people, were arrested. Famous Communists were often persuaded or tortured into confessing to all sorts of 'crimes' such as sabotage, working as agents for Trotsky or spying for Germany. Then they confessed to their 'crimes' in public **show trials** before being found guilty and shot. The biggest show trials were held in 1936 and 1938, and were well publicised. The victims included Zinoviev, Kamenev and Bukharin, who had all been close to Lenin and rivals of Stalin in the 1920s. Two heads of the secret police, Yagoda and Yezhov, were also purged.

D The historian R Hingley describes Stalin's methods in *Joseph Stalin: Man and Legend* (1974).

> The Zinoviev trial was an act of murder performed by Stalin. From the start the rigging of the trial was closely planned by Stalin in person. He had many ways of making his victims talk. Held in isolation for months or even years on end, deprived of sleep, beaten night and day, the defendants were usually more than half broken already when confronted with the signed confessions of associates previously brainwashed. Stalin would shout that Zinoviev and Kamenev were to be 'given the works' until they came crawling on their bellies with confessions in their teeth. Zinoviev was influenced by threats to his family, being also subjected to the physical ordeal of a cell deliberately overheated in the height of summer … The dictator did, however, give his personal word that neither Zinoviev nor Kamenev would be executed if they would stand trial on his terms. It was on the basis of this lying assurance that the two chief victims finally went to their doom.

The Muslims, millions of whom lived in the Central Asian regions of the USSR, also suffered during the purges. During the 1920s they had been tolerated more than the Russian Christians. But, after Stalin's rise to power, they were persecuted: many mosques were closed and Muslim women were encouraged to remove their veils. Muslim practices, such as the pilgrimage to Mecca, were forbidden. In some areas there was widespread revolt against the government.

Stalin continued to urge stronger measures. He declared: 'We must not lull the Party but sharpen its vigilance; we must not lull it to sleep but keep it ready for action; not disarm it but arm it.'

C The top photograph shows Stalin with police chief Yezhov on the right, alongside the Moscow–Volga Canal. The bottom photograph shows the same picture altered, after Yezhov had been purged.

E A French view of life in Soviet Russia. The caption on the poster reads 'We are very happy'.

In 1937 thousands of Red Army officers were shot for treason. The victims included the army leader and Civil War hero Marshal Tukhachevsky. The Soviet army was seriously weakened at a critical time just before the war with Germany.

Ordinary victims of the purges disappeared much more quietly. They were killed or sent to labour camps. In 1935 one million people in Moscow and Leningrad alone were executed. Millions of others followed them.

Over one third of Communist Party members were arrested between 1934 and 1939, and probably two thirds of these were executed.

F Extracts from Alexander Solzhenitsyn's *Gulag Archipelago* (1986). Solzhenitsyn himself spent many years in a Stalinist labour camp.

(i) A district party conference was under way in Moscow Province ... A tribute to Comrade Stalin was called for. The small hall echoed with stormy applause rising to an ovation: for three minutes, four minutes, five minutes ... The older people were panting from exhaustion. The applause went on six, seven, eight minutes. The NKVD were watching to see who quit first.

The director of the local paper factory aware of all the falsity [lack of honesty] sat down after eleven minutes. And, oh what a miracle took place, where had all the enthusiasm gone? To a man everyone else stopped dead and sat down.

That same night the paper factory director was arrested. His interrogator told him, 'Don't ever be the first to stop applauding.'

(ii) A woman was going home late one night ... she passed some people working to free a truck that had got stuck. It turned out to be full of corpses - hands and legs stuck out from beneath the canvas. They wrote down her name and the next day she was arrested. The interrogator asked her what she had seen. She told him truthfully. She was sentenced to ten years for anti-Soviet agitation.

G The secret police.

The secret police was Stalin's instrument for carrying out the Terror. After the revolution Lenin had created the Cheka. It was replaced by the GPU and the OGPU (United State Political Administration) in 1924. Later this became the NKVD (the People's Commissariat for Internal Affairs) – the force which carried out the purges of the 1930s

Some of the victims may have been guilty of crimes. But most were innocent. The purges created a sense of hysteria.

> A woman was sentenced to ten years in a prison camp for saying, after his arrest, that Tukhachevsky was handsome.

People were encouraged to accuse others in order to demonstrate their own loyalty to the Party. Children were even encouraged to inform on their parents if they seemed unenthusiastic about what Stalin was doing. Some people accused others in order to get their jobs. Even to know a foreign language could get you arrested as an 'enemy spy'. If someone was arrested, their families and friends automatically became suspects also.

Stalin's motives

Why did Stalin allow such terror? Some people think he was simply mad. But he was certainly suspicious of possible rivals. Perhaps he wanted Soviet citizens to feel insecure and therefore less likely to challenge him. The purges were also a convenient way of excusing failures and setbacks. For example, failures to achieve targets under the Five-year Plans could be blamed on sabotage rather than faults in the Plans.

Stalin signed many death warrants himself. Stalin appeared to be in complete control and, when he felt more secure in 1939, he relaxed the terror.

H Jokes told in the USSR in the 1930s.

(i) Stalin wanted to get a true picture of what people thought of him, so he went in disguise into a cinema. After the main film, a newsreel was shown with Stalin in every scene. All the audience stood up and loudly applauded. Stalin stayed modestly seated. After a few moments the man next to Stalin nudged him and said quietly, 'Most people feel the same way as you, comrade. But it would be safer if you stood up.'

(ii) A flock of sheep was stopped by frontier guards at the Russo–Finnish border.
'Why do you want to leave Russia?' the guards asked.
'It's the NKVD [the Soviet secret police],' replied the terrified sheep. 'Beria [head of the NKVD] has ordered them to arrest all elephants.'
'But you're not elephants!' the guards exclaimed.
'Yes,' said the sheep. 'But try telling that to the NKVD!'

The cult of personality

The Terror went hand-in-hand with a cult of personality. Soviet propaganda presented Stalin as a god-like figure. His name and picture were everywhere. Streets and cities were named after him, poems and plays were written about him. History books were re-written to make Stalin seem the most important man in Russia after Lenin, even at the time of the revolution.

I A propaganda painting by a Soviet artist, showing Stalin meeting ordinary people.

Q

1 What did it mean to be 'purged' in the USSR in (i) the 1920s and (ii) the 1930s?
2 Why was Kirov's murder in 1934 important?
3 a) What was a show trial?
   b) Why were some important Communists given show trials?
4 Why was source C altered by the Soviet government?
5 The historian in source D shows Stalin as a ruthless murderer but source I shows him to be popular with the people. How can you explain this difference in interpretation?
6 What message is the cartoonist in source E trying to get across?
7 What can you learn from sources G and H about life and attitudes during the purges? Are they reliable evidence? Can jokes be useful evidence?
8 What was Stalin's cult of personality? Why do you think he encouraged it?
9 Use all the evidence in this chapter to decide why Stalin carried out the purges. Did he achieve what he wanted?

Life in Stalin's USSR

Key Issues **What was life like for citizens of the USSR in the 1930s? Had their lives improved since the revolution?**

Earlier chapters have shown how life for most people in the Soviet Union in the 1930s was difficult and insecure. How did ordinary people cope?

The Communist Party

Almost everybody would have known someone who suffered in the purges, even if they escaped themselves. But some people actually did quite well. They would have belonged to the Communist Party. It was necessary to have the support of the Party to do well in any job. The Party had a list of over one million approved members, considered reliable. The list was called the *Nomenklatura*. When an important job became vacant, somebody from this list would be appointed. Although many Party members were purged during the 1930s, there was always somebody to take their place.

In order to join the Party, you had to be approved by at least two other existing members. Then you had to serve a trial period before becoming a full member. Being a Party member carried responsibilities. For example, you had to give up spare time to attend meetings and explain Party policy to your workmates.

Some Party members became full-time officials. Those who reached a certain level got special privileges, such as being able to buy things in shops which were not open to the general population.

The soviets were elected by the whole population in regular elections. But there was usually no choice between candidates, who were often Communist Party members. The soviets had very limited powers. Real power lay with the Party. Party members were not elected, but were chosen to attend committees and congresses. Important decisions were made by the Central Committee and the Politburo, but at the height of Stalin's power, not even the Politburo met regularly. Important decisions were made by Stalin and his appointed advisers.

Women in the USSR

The lives of some groups of people had been considerably altered since the revolution. One such group was women. Traditionally in Russia they had always been second-class citizens, with few

Stalin

State/government	Party
	Politburo
Council of Ministers	Central Committee
Supreme Soviet	Party Congress (met every five years)
Soviets of republics	Republic central Party committees
Provincial, regional and area soviets (numbering 146)	Provincial, regional and area committees (numbering 146)
City and district soviets (numbering 4500)	City and district Party committees (numbering 4500)
Village and local soviets (about 40 000)	Local Party groups (about 420 000)

A Power in the state and party.

rights. The Communist Party declared that they were equal to men. In parts of the Soviet Union, particularly the Muslim republics in Asia, women received more personal freedom than ever before.

B A woman worker in a tractor factory.

However, life remained very hard for most Soviet women. Some took on jobs like engineering which had once only been done by men. But there was a shortage of workers, and most women were expected to work full time as well as looking after homes. Less than 20 per cent of the Communist Party was made up of women. Very few women rose to high positions in the Party or government.

Women were also encouraged to have more children. Because there was a shortage of workers, those who had large families received special rewards. In the 1920s the government had made divorce easy. A law in 1936 changed this. Abortion was also made illegal, and more benefits were given to families.

Children

Children gained from the revolution in some ways. Before 1917 a large number never attended school. After the revolution many schools were built. But schools were very disciplined, especially after an education law in 1935. Teachers were expected to teach only the Communist view, and there was no free discussion. School uniforms were brought back and pupils had to learn by heart rules such as that in source C. Many children joined Communist Party youth organisations.

> The Communist Party tried to influence young people through its youth movements. There were the Young Octobrists for 8–11 year-olds; the Pioneers for 11 year-olds; and the Komsomol for those over 16.

C A rule of education.

It is the duty of each school child to acquire knowledge persistently so as to become an educated and cultured citizen and to be of the greatest possible service to his country.

Religion

Religion had always been important in Russia. But all organised religions suffered in the USSR in the 1920s and 1930s. As well as churches being closed, religious worship was condemned as taking people's attention away from what was important: life in the here and now. Over five million members of the League of Militant Atheists spread anti-religious propaganda and tried to prevent people attending those churches that survived.

Censorship

All books, newspapers, the radio and films were censored. Only the official Communist Party viewpoint was allowed. The Party preached that it was service to the state, not freedom of the individual, that was all important. Since it was claimed that the Party ran things for the benefit of everybody, anyone who was suspected of acting 'individually', or who criticised the state or Party, was thought to be committing treason.

> In the 1937 census 50 million Russians were still prepared to state that they had religious beliefs – but this fact was not published.

Russians and non-Russians

Non-Russians in other republics of the USSR had particularly difficult lives. Stalin distrusted national groups which might be disloyal to his regime. He tried to make people see themselves as 'Soviet citizens' rather than Russians, Ukrainians and so on. Non-Russian languages and traditions were often discouraged. But it was mostly Russians who had the top positions in the Party and the government.

Some people certainly did well out of Stalin's changes in the economy, the Party and life generally. There were new jobs to be had, and some people were able to make good from very ordinary backgrounds. All citizens were certainly told that their lives were better than ever before. But there were also many shortages, and living conditions in both the overcrowded towns and the collectivised countryside were hard for most people.

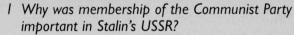

Q

1 Why was membership of the Communist Party important in Stalin's USSR?

2 Look again at the evidence in this chapter and Chapters 16, 17 and 18. For each of the following groups, decide whether their lives had improved or not during the 1930s:
   a) Party members
   b) women
   c) children
   d) farmworkers
   e) factory workers
   f) members of churches
   g) non-Russian citizens of the USSR.

It is important to remember that many people would have belonged to more than one group.

20

The Arts and Propaganda

How were the arts and propaganda used in the Soviet Union to put across the Communist point of view?

Communists believed that most things, including art and literature, had reflected the interests of the ruling class before the revolution. Therefore they assumed that new forms of art would develop after 1917. Many artists, writers and musicians did try out new ideas after the revolution. But much of the new art and films were used as propaganda to get across a political message. Propaganda ships and trains were sent across the USSR to spread new 'proletarian culture'.

Socialist realism

All art had to have a political purpose. Even before Lenin's death, the freedom of artists, writers and musicians to experiment was restricted. But this became far more severe under Stalin. Famous composers like Prokoviev were told to write music that could be easily understood by ordinary people.

A A worker and a woman collective farmer – an example of socialist realist sculpture from 1937.

Stalin favoured 'socialist realism'. This meant that writers and artists were expected to show happy and heroic workers, working for the victory of Communism. The bad side of life was never shown.

The sources in this chapter all show examples of propaganda.

B Lenin on the Tribune, 1930.

C An ode to Stalin on his sixtieth birthday by the composer Prokoviev (1939).

Never have our fertile fields such a harvest shown,
Never have our villages such contentment known.
Never life has been so fair, spirits been so high,
Never to the present day grew so green the rye.
O'er the earth the rising sun sheds a warmer light,
Since it looked on Stalin's face it has grown more bright.
I am singing to my baby sleeping in my arms,
Grow like flowers in the meadow free from all alarm.
On your lips the name of Stalin will protect from harm.
You will learn the source of sunshine bathing all our land.
You will copy Stalin's portrait with your tiny hand.

J V Stalin is the genius, the leader and teacher of the Party, the greatest strategist of Socialist revolution, helmsman of the Soviet State and captain of armies … His work is extraordinary for its variety; his energy truly amazing … everyone is familiar with the invincible force of Stalin's logic, the crystal clarity of his mind, his iron will, his devotion to the Party, his ardent faith in the people, and love for the people. Everybody is familiar with his modesty, his simplicity of manner, his consideration for people, and his merciless severity towards enemies of the people … Stalin is the worthy continuer of the cause of Lenin, or, as it is said in the Party: Stalin is the Lenin of today.

F A poster from 1935 showing Stalin and Voroshilov, head of the armed forces. It reads 'Long Live the Red Workers and Peasants' Army, Loyal Guardians of the Soviet Frontiers'.

E 'All of Moscow is building the Metro' – a poster from 1934. Kaganovich, the head of the Moscow Party organisation, is pictured at the top. The Moscow underground system was one of the great building achievements of the 1930s.

What impact did the Second World War have on the USSR?

In Germany Hitler had long made it clear that he intended eventually to invade the USSR. His aim was to destroy Communism and turn Russia into a German colony. Stalin managed to keep out of the Second World War whilst Germany fought against Britain and France in 1939 and 1940, but Germany was ready to attack the USSR in 1941. Yet the massive invasion, when it came in June 1941, still appeared to take Stalin by surprise.

The German attack on the USSR

The German attack made rapid progress into Russia. Soon the Germans occupied huge areas of Soviet territory, and had killed or captured millions of Soviet soldiers.

At first there were some people, for example in the Ukraine, who welcomed the Germans. They hoped that they would be freed from Communism and that unpopular policies like collectivisation would be scrapped. But Hitler regarded the Soviet peoples as inferior, and the Germans treated them cruelly, losing possible support. Many Russians became **partisans**, fighting on against the Germans in occupied territory.

Stalin soon recovered his nerve after the first German attacks. He began a policy of all-out war against the Germans. Early on, whole factories were dismantled and taken on trains east of the Ural mountains, to be reassembled beyond the range of German bombers. In July 1941 26 armaments factories were moved from the Moscow and Leningrad regions alone.

B An extract from a Soviet school textbook, published in 1976.

Zina Portnova was a young Pioneer [a member of the Communist youth movement] … Zina became a partisan. One day, when out on an assignment, she was captured. The officer questioning her brandished a pistol at her and then put it down on his desk. She grabbed it and shot the officer dead. With a second shot she killed another officer. Then she smashed the window with her boot and killed the sentry outside. She pressed the trigger for the fourth time but the pistol failed her and she was captured again. She was horribly tortured by the Nazis but she died as she had lived – a real heroine.

The entire Soviet population was mobilised for war. Those men not in the army, women and children worked in the factories or helped to dig huge tank traps and other defences. By 1943 the Soviets were producing more war material than the Germans. They were also helped by supplies from their American and British allies.

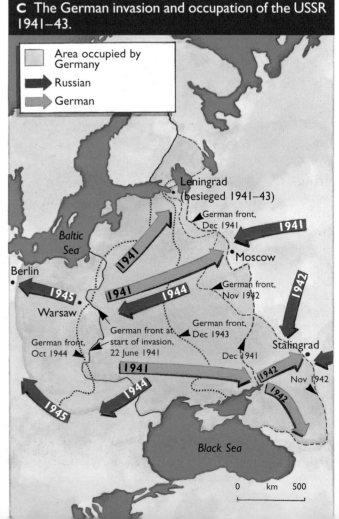

C The German invasion and occupation of the USSR 1941–43.

- Area occupied by Germany
- Russian
- German

Leningrad (besieged 1941–43)
German front, Dec 1941
1941
Baltic Sea
1941
Moscow
Berlin
1945
1941
1944
German front, Nov 1942
1942
Warsaw
German front, Oct 1944
German front at start of invasion, 22 June 1941
German front, Dec 1943
Dec 1941
Stalingrad
German front, Dec 1941
1941
1942
Nov 1942
1944
1942
1945
Black Sea
0 km 500

A German soldiers executing Soviet partisans in 1941.

D 'The Motherland Calls.' A Soviet recruiting poster from 1941.

The Soviet fightback

The German attack was halted at the end of 1941 outside Moscow and Leningrad. The Germans ran into problems with the winter weather, but were also stopped by the heroic resistance of the Soviets. The Germans attacked again in 1942, but at the end of the year were defeated at the Battle of Stalingrad, one of the turning points of the war. From 1943 onwards the Red Army gradually pushed the Germans back into their own country. Soviet troops entered Berlin in the spring of 1945, Hitler committed suicide and the Germans surrendered.

The impact of war

The Soviet victory was a great achievement. But the people had suffered enormously. The Germans had caused massive destruction during their attacks and occupation. The Soviets had destroyed some of their own land as they retreated, so that it would be of no use to the Germans. Many of the achievements of the Five-year Plans were destroyed.

Between 1941 and 1944 the Germans had laid siege to the city of Leningrad. They never captured it, but during the siege the city lost one third of its inhabitants, many through starvation and disease.

Despite the devastation, the USSR emerged from the war along with America as a superpower. Stalin had wartime conferences with the American and British leaders. He was now an international statesman as well as Soviet leader.

Stalin used every means to inspire his people. He appealed to them to fight for 'Mother Russia' rather than for Communism. Even churches were re-opened so that people could pray for victory.

Stalin was in total control. He proved to be an inspiring leader, although he did make some mistakes. He chose able generals like Marshal Zhukov. He was also as ruthless as ever in his treatment of those he distrusted. Whole national groups were shifted from one part of the country to another if Stalin had any doubts about their loyalty.

E 'How have you Helped the Front?'

F Entries from the diary of Tanya Savcheva, a young girl in Leningrad.

1941
Zhenya died on December 28, 12.30 in the morning.

1942
Babushka [Grandmother] died on January 25, 3 o'clock.
Leka died on March 17, 5 o'clock in the morning.
Dedya Vasya died on April 13, 2 o'clock at night.
Dedya Lisha on May 10, 4 o'clock in the afternoon.
Mama died on May 13, 7.30 am.

Svichevs died. All died. Only Tanya remains.

Q

1 Why did the Germans invade the USSR in 1941?
2 What was the message of sources D and E?
3 What clues do sources A, B and F give about the nature of the war in the USSR and the people's reaction to it?

The USSR During Stalin's Last Years, 1945–53

To what extent had the USSR recovered from the Second World War by 1953? How did Stalin run the USSR after the war?

The price of victory

The USSR was a victorious country in 1945, but the price of victory had been very high:

- probably nearly nine million Soviet soldiers died and 18 million were wounded;
- nearly six million Soviet soldiers taken prisoner;
- about 19 million Soviet civilians died during the war;
- over 1700 towns and 70 000 villages destroyed;
- over 31 000 factories were destroyed;
- 65 000 kilometres of railway line were destroyed;
- 40 000 hospitals, 84 000 schools and 43 000 libraries were destroyed;
- seven million horses, 17 million cattle, 20 million pigs and 27 million sheep and goats were killed or taken to Germany.

A A Russian man and boy return to their ruined village at the end of the war.

> **B** Ilya Ehrenburg, a Russian, recalls his optimism after the war in *The War 1941–45* (1965).
>
> I firmly believed that after victory everything would suddenly change … everybody expected that once victory had been won, people would know real happiness. We realised, of course, that the country had been devastated, impoverished, that we would have to work hard, and we did not have fantasies about mountains of gold. But we believed that victory would bring justice, that human dignity would triumph.

Recovery after the war

The USSR's main aim in 1945, therefore, was to recover from the devastation caused by four years of total war. A massive programme of reconstruction began with the Fourth Five-year Plan. By 1950 some of the production figures were back to pre-war levels. As well as relying on their own efforts, the Soviets took much industrial material from Germany and eastern Europe and rebuilt it in the USSR.

Serious problems remained. Much housing had been damaged during the War, and there was overcrowding in the cities. Food and consumer goods were still in short supply. The population found life hard. Taxes were raised and collective farms had to provide more food for the government.

C The Fourth Five-year Plan 1946–50.

	1945	1950 (figures planned in 1945)	1950 (actual figures in 1950)
Coal (million tonnes)	147.3	250.0	261.1
Steel (million tonnes)	12.3	25.4	27.3
Pig-iron (million tonnes)	8.8	19.5	19.2
Oil (million tonnes)	19.4	35.4	37.9
Cement (million tonnes)	1.8	10.5	10.2
Workers (millions)	27.3	33.5	39.2

D A poster from 1947. It reads: 'Work hard during harvest time and you'll be rewarded with plenty of bread.'

Cold War

After Germany's defeat the USSR and its western allies, Britain and America, became more and more suspicious of each other. They had little in common now that Germany had been defeated. Soon a state of tension or 'Cold War' existed between them, and in the next few years alliances were created to protect their interests in Europe: NATO (the North Atlantic Treaty Organisation) in western Europe, and the Warsaw Pact in eastern Europe. Stalin made sure that there were Communist governments in control in eastern Europe, so that the Soviets themselves felt more secure.

Stalin remained very suspicious of the west. At the end of the war many people in the USSR hoped that things would become more relaxed. But Stalin's rule was as harsh as ever. Many Soviet soldiers and civilians were imprisoned for no other crime than having been in contact with foreigners during the war. Foreign influences were still kept out of the USSR.

Stalin's last years

Stalin's health was less good after the war. He made only two more speeches, and never appeared in public. He was as suspicious of his colleagues as ever. Although the purges now were not on the same scale as those of the 1930s, the secret police was still active in arresting suspects. The head of the secret police, Lavrenti Beria, was as feared as Stalin.

Stalin himself appeared more powerful than ever. After 1947 he did not even allow the Central Committee and Politburo to meet. He ruled as an absolute dictator. He also began a new campaign of terror. In 1949 he began a purge of the Communist Party in Leningrad. In spite of the heroic defence of Leningrad during the war, thousands of Party members there were rounded up, accused of disloyalty, and shot. Stalin even had his own sisters-in-law arrested in 1949.

Stalin's last purge was aimed at Jews. Jews in Russia had often suffered from persecution before the revolution, because of prejudice and their different religion. These attacks had mostly stopped, and many leading Party members had been Jewish, including Trotsky. But a 'Doctors' Plot' was announced in 1953. Jewish doctors at a Moscow clinic used by Soviet leaders were accused of plotting to poison Stalin. It appears that Stalin was just about to begin another bloody purge, when he died in March 1953.

> Before Stalin's death, two whole national groups – the Volga Germans and the Crimean Tartars – were moved to Siberia because Stalin believed that they had been sympathetic to the Germans during the war.

E Stalin lying in state, 1953.

1 Explain briefly what was meant by 'The price of victory had been very high' for the USSR.
2 Why was the author of source B optimistic? Were his hopes justified?
3 Look at source C. How successfully did the USSR recover from the war by 1950?
4 What was the Cold War, and why did it break out?
5 What were the Leningrad purge and the 'Doctors' Plot'?
6 Did Stalin's way of ruling the USSR change after the war compared to before the war? Consider both the economy and the treatment of the Soviet people.

When Stalin died in 1953 there was no single obvious person to follow him as leader. At first there was a '**collective leadership**' of several leading Communist Party members. The greatly feared head of the secret police, Beria, was quickly arrested and executed.

The rise of Khrushchev

Many people thought that Malenkov, the Prime Minister, would become the next leader. But Nikita Khrushchev was in charge of the party and also had the support of the army generals. By 1956 Khrushchev had pushed his rivals aside. Unlike in Stalin's day, they were not put on trial and executed, but given other and less important jobs. People began to feel more secure.

Khrushchev was very different from Stalin, although he also came from a humble background. Khrushchev liked to be popular with people and was very outgoing. He travelled widely both inside and outside the USSR, listening to complaints and meeting a wide range of people. He recognised that there were things in the USSR that could be changed for the better. He said that his aim was to make the USSR a genuinely Communist country within 20 years. He also boasted that the Soviets would be better off than people in the capitalist west.

The attack on Stalin's memory

In 1956 Khrushchev felt strong enough to make the first serious attack on Stalin's reputation. The attack was made in the so-called 'secret speech' at the Twentieth Party Congress. Although Khrushchev said that Stalin had achieved many things, he also accused Stalin of having acted illegally and brutally towards the Soviet people. Khrushchev attacked Stalin's cult of personality. However, he said little about the part played by Party members like himself in carrying out Stalin's wishes. He preferred to put the blame on Stalin rather than suggest that there might be something really wrong with the Soviet system itself.

After 1956 nearly eight million prisoners were released, and six million people who had been killed during Stalin's rule were declared innocent of any crime.

A An extract from Khrushchev's secret speech of 1956.

> It was during the period 1935-8 that the practice of mass repression ... was born, first against the enemies of Leninism – Trotskyites, Zinovievites and Bukharinites ... and subsequently against many honest Communists ...
>
> Stalin began the idea of 'enemy of the people' ... Stalin was a very distrustful man, sickly suspicious; we knew this from our work with him ... The sickly suspicion created in him a general distrust even towards important party workers he had known for years. Everywhere and in everything he saw 'enemies', 'two-facers' and 'spies'.

B A story from Khrushchev's time.

> At the Twentieth Party Congress Khrushchev was listing Stalin's crimes when a voice came from the back of the hall: 'And where were you then?'
> 'Would the man who asked that question stand up,' said Khrushchev.
> Nobody stood up.
> 'That's where we were, too!' replied Khrushchev.

De-Stalinisation

Khrushchev wanted to make some changes in the USSR, and this was one reason for his attack on Stalin, the start of '**de-Stalinisation**'. Several changes were certainly made:

- there was less censorship and it was possible to criticise in writing some things Stalin had done;
- the activities of the secret police were restricted;
- attempts were made to help the peasants and make farming more efficient;
- there was less central planning, and attempts were made to make industry more efficient.

However, de-Stalinisation was strictly limited. There was no effort to seriously limit the powers of the Communist Party, and no real changes to the system. There was also a lot of opposition to any changes from some people in the Party. Khrushchev himself faced an attempt by some of his colleagues to sack him in 1957. He had to bring his supporters from all over the USSR to Moscow in order to outvote his rivals on the Central Committee. However, it was clear that the Communist Party was not going to allow a leader to have the same amount of power as Stalin had

C Khrushchev being greeted by the head of a collective farm in Moldavia, 1959.

D Stalin's statue being pulled down in Budapest (the capital of Hungary) in 1956.

held. In 1964, when Khrushchev's policies were seen to have failed, he was sacked as leader and allowed to retire peacefully. Lenin and Stalin would never have allowed that to happen!

Trouble in eastern Europe

Khrushchev's attack on Stalin had some unexpected results elsewhere. In some of the eastern European Communist countries which had copied Stalin's system, people began to make demands for more changes. They were encouraged by what Khrushchev was doing in the USSR. This happened particularly in Poland and Hungary. But when the Hungarian government allowed anti-Soviet demonstrations, Soviet troops invaded the Hungarian capital Budapest. The Soviets were afraid that Hungary would leave the Soviet alliance. The 1956 Hungarian Rising was brutally crushed. It was clear that de-Stalinisation had limits and that the soviets were not prepared to risk losing control of eastern Europe.

After Khrushchev

Stalin's death was still recent. Although his memory was now being attacked, there were few people in the Party in the USSR who were prepared to consider big changes at this time. It was to be another generation before such changes in the Soviet system were seriously considered. Khrushchev's successor as leader was Leonid Brezhnev. He made very few changes, even though the USSR began to have many difficulties, especially with its economy. The Soviet people were constantly told that their way of doing things was still the best. The influence of Stalin lived on.

Q

1 a) What was the message of Khrushchev's 'secret speech' of 1956?
  b) Why was this speech important?
2 What point is being made in the story in source B?
3 a) What was meant by 'de-Stalinisation'?
  b) What did de-Stalinisation mean for the USSR?
  c) What did de-Stalinisation mean for eastern Europe?
4 Did Khrushchev succeed in changing much in the USSR? What difficulties did he come up against?

Extended writing
Think again about what you have studied in this book. How much had the lives of the Soviet people changed by 1956 compared to before the November 1917 Revolution? Were their lives better or worse? It might help you if you draw and complete a table like the one opposite before arriving at your answer.

	Russia before November Revolution	USSR In 1956	Change for better or worse
Economy	Industry privately owned; land mostly owned by rich landowners		
Political system	Several political parties; no censorship; individual freedoms after March Revolution		
Position in the world	Russia not regarded as a modern, advanced country; not a leading world power		

Stalin and Stalinism

What is Stalin's reputation? Has it changed? What did Stalin achieve?

During his 25 years in power Stalin changed the USSR from a relatively backward country into a great industrial power. Then he led the USSR to victory in the Second World War. The USSR emerged from the war as a superpower. But during Stalin's rule millions of Soviet citizens died, either because of Stalin's actions or because of the war. Some people have called Stalin the greatest mass murderer in history. But many Russians admired his strong leadership.

Stalin's influence lasted long after his death. The USSR which he created continued for almost 40 years after his death before Communism was overthrown. There were some changes after Stalin: for example there were no more large-scale purges. But not much else changed until General Secretary Gorbachev came to power in 1985.

Opinions about Stalin have varied a lot. Whilst he was alive, only very flattering things could be said about him in the USSR. His way of running the country became known as 'Stalinism', and despite what Khrushchev attempted in the 1950s, it lasted for a long time not just in the USSR but also in other Communist countries.

The following sources show some of the ways in which Stalin was regarded inside and outside his own country.

A Two of the last photographs of Stalin: *(above)* Stalin and his children in the 1930s, and *(below)* Stalin in 1949.

B Leon Trotsky on Stalin in 1940:

Undoubtedly characteristic of Stalin is personal, physical cruelty, what is usually called sadism ... After he had become a Soviet leader, he would amuse himself in his country home, by cutting the throats of sheep or pouring petrol on ant heaps and setting fire to them.

C Stalin's daughter Svetlana Alliluyeva writing about her father in *Only One Year* (1969):

He gave his name to this bloodbath of absolute dictatorship. He knew what he was doing. He was neither insane nor misled. With cold calculation he had cemented his own power, afraid of losing it more than anything else in the world.

D The Russian historian Roy Medvedev in his book *On Stalin and Stalinism* (1979):

He lived very modestly in a Kremlin apartment formerly occupied by a palace servant. He always wore simple clothes and had little taste for luxury or other creature comforts ... He was a strong-willed man who nevertheless remained extremely cautious and at times even indecisive ... The overwhelming passion of his life was power, yet he could be patient and bide his time before striking a blow at political rivals.

E A British historian's opinion of Stalin (from *Joseph Stalin* by Alan Jamieson, 1971):

Under his inspiration Russia has modernised her society and educated her masses ... Stalin found Russia working with a wooden plough and left her equipped with nuclear power.

F The British cartoonist Vicky produced a humorous imaginary version of Stalin's 'Testament' based on Lenin's famous 'Testament' from the 1920s.

H 'The verdict of history' – a poster from 1988. Although Stalin was long dead, there was a suggestion that Stalin should face a firing squad, as a punishment for the crimes he committed whilst alive.

As Communism came under attack in the USSR in the 1980s, there was a lot of interest in what had happened under Stalin and how the truth had been hidden. Sources G and H show this.

G 'Requiem' – another poster from 1988. During the 1930s, thousands of victims had been transported to prison camps in Kazakhstan, Siberia and the Soviet Far East.

Q

1 How might the two photographs in source A have been used as pro-Stalinist propaganda?
2 Are sources D and E more in favour of Stalin or against him? Explain your answer.
3 'Source F is humorous, but it is also trying to make a serious point.' Do you agree? Explain your answer.
4 What messages are sources G and H trying to put across?
5 Sources B and E have different views about Stalin. What reasons can you give to explain these different interpretations?

Extended writing
'Stalin was a great leader who made the Soviet Union a modern, world power and led it to victory in the Second World War.' Do you agree with this view? Explain your answer using the evidence in this and other chapters.

Glossary

abdicate – when a king or queen gives up their throne

autocracy – a political system in which one person (an autocrat) has absolute or total power

Bolsheviks – members of the Social Democrats, who, led by Lenin, believed that a revolutionary party must be disciplined, secretive and led by dedicated, professional leaders

bourgeoisie – middle class. The word was often used by Communists to describe capitalists or people who were wealthy

boycott – to deliberately have nothing to do with someone or something

capitalists – usually business people or other well off people who own businesses or property

censorship – the process of keeping information out of books, newspapers, films etc in order to keep it secret from the public

collective leadership – when there is no single ruler in charge, and a country is run by several people who co-operate with each other

commissars – Communist Party officials; sometimes government ministers

conscription – the practice of requiring all young men in a country to serve a period of time in the army

constituency – a geographical area in which the inhabitants vote for an individual to represent them

deputy – member of parliament

despotism – a political system like autocracy in which one person rules, usually very harshly

de-Stalinisation – a process by which methods associated with Stalin's rule were deliberately changed (after his death)

Duma – the Russian word for parliament

faction – a small, organised, dissenting group within a larger group

imperialists – a word used as a term of abuse by Communists, to refer to capitalists and those seeking to wage war and gain more territory

inflation – when prices and wages rise rapidly and money loses its value

Komsomol – the Communist Party youth movement

Kulaks – wealthy peasants or farmers

Mensheviks – members of the Social Democrats who, unlike Lenin and the Bolsheviks, believed in a less secretive party and a more gradual approach to revolution

middle class – usually those people who are comfortably off, but not as rich as the upper class; often professional people

mutiny – a revolt by soldiers who refuse to obey their officers or the government

nationalised – when a government takes over privately owned businesses and property

partisans – civilians who carry on fighting against an enemy occupying their country in wartime, even when the army has been defeated

privatised – when land or industry owned by the government or state is sold back to private owners

proletariat – the name given by Communists to working-class people living in towns, especially factory workers

propaganda – using books, films etc to persuade people to believe certain things, often exaggerating them or lying to get across a particular point of view

requisition – when the government forcibly takes food or property from people, usually in wartime

ruling class – those rich or powerful people from whom the leaders of a country are drawn

show trials – a propaganda trial staged by the government and deliberately fixed to make sure that its opponents are found guilty

soviet – the Russian word for council

Acknowledgements

The front cover is a portrait of Stalin, reproduced courtesy of the David King Collection.

The Publishers would like to thank the following for permission to reproduce material in this volume:

Anchor Foundation for extracts from *From Lenin to Stalin* by D V Serge (1973); Bell for the extract from *Joseph Stalin* by A Jamieson (1971); Collins Harvill for extracts from *The Gulag Archipelago* by A Solzhenitsyn (1986); HarperCollins for extracts from *Stalin* by Trotsky (1941); Hutchinson for the extract from *Joseph Stalin: Man and Legend* by R Hingley (1974) reprinted by permission of the Peters Fraser and Dunlop Group Ltd; *On Stalin and Stalinism* by Medvedev (translated by Ellen de Kadt) (1979) by permission of Oxford University Press; Penguin for extracts from *Ten Days That Shook the World* by John Reed (1977) and *An Economic History of the USSR* by A Nove (1972); Phoenix Press for the extract from *The Russian Tragedy* by Alexander Berkman (1986); Progress Publishers for the extract from 'By Lenin's Study' by Alexander Yashin (translated by Peter Tempest) (1956) and for the extract from *History of the USSR* by Y Kukushkin (1981); the Novosti Press Agency for extracts from *Early Russia – The USSR* by T Golubeva and L Gellerstein (1976); an extract from *The Times* © Times Newspapers, 1924; the 'Ode to Stalin on his Sixtieth Birthday' by Prokoviev was originally quoted in *Russia at War* by A Werth (Barrie and Rockcliff, 1954); the quote from Tanya Savcheva's diary originally appeared in *Russia* by J Nichol and K Shepherd (Basil Blackwell, 1986).

The Publishers would also like to thank the following for permission to reproduce copyright illustrations in this volume:

Archiv Gerstenberg p.46ar; The David King Collection pp. 5, 7, 8, 9, 11, 17, 18, 19, 23, 24, 25, 26, 29, 31, 33, 34b, 36, 37, 38, 41, 42a, 43bl, 45, 46br, 46rb, 47, 49, 52, 53, 54, 55, 56l, 57, 60; Hulton Getty pp. 13, 15, 32; Mary Evans Picture Library p.21a; Novosti (London) pp. 21b, 34a, 35a, 40, 52bl; Popperfoto pp. 12l, 50; Punch p. 4; SCR Photo Library pp.12 r, 42b, 43ar and br, 56r, 61bl and ar; UKC/Stephen Brasher, New Statesman p.61al, Topham p.43l (**a** above; **b** below; **l** left; **r** right)

Every effort has been made to trace and acknowledge ownership of copyright. The publishers will be glad to make suitable arrangements with any copyright holders whom it has not been possible to contact.

In memory of John Aylett, who devised this series.

British Library Cataloguing in Publication Data
A catalogue record for this title is available from the British Library
ISBN 0–340–62024-2

First published in 1997
Impression number 10 9 8 7 6 5 4 3 2 1
Year 2002 2001 2000 1999 1998 1997

Typeset by GreenGate Publishing Services, Tonbridge, Kent.

Printed for Hodder and Stoughton Educational, a division of Hodder Headline Plc, 338 Euston Road, London NW1 3BH by Colorcraft Ltd, Hong Kong.